# Computer Viruses

What they are
How they work
How to avoid them

*Jonathan L. Mayo*

*To Mom and*
*Granny Nell*

Windcrest books are published by Windcrest Books, an imprint of TAB BOOKS.
The name "Windcrest" is a registered trademark of TAB BOOKS.

FIRST EDITION
THIRD PRINTING

**Library of Congress Cataloging-in-Publication Data**

Mayo, Jonathan L.
    Computer viruses : what they are, how they work, and how to avoid
them / by Jonathan L. Mayo.

        p.      cm.
    Includes index.
    ISBN 0-8306-9582-6      ISBN 0-8306-3382-0 (pbk.)
    1. Computer viruses.   I. Title.
QA76.76.C68M33   1989
005.8—dc20                                          89-33481
                                                      CIP

TAB BOOKS offers software for sale. For information and a catalog, please contact
TAB Software Department, Blue Ridge Summit, PA 17294-0850.

Questions regarding the content of this book should be addressed to:

**Reader Inquiry Branch**
**Windcrest Books**
**Blue Ridge Summit, PA 17294-0850**

Cover Photograph: A model of a DNA supercoil having 171 base pairs—some 7000 atoms
(Courtesy of Lawrence Livermore National Laboratory).

Illustrations for Chapter Openings are adapted from Cyclopedia of Universal History, Vol. I.,
by John Clark Ridpath, LL.D., (John T. Jones, 1885)

• The Wooden Horse
• The Pythia on the Tripod, drawn by H. Levteman.
• Genseric's Warriors Plundering a Camp, drawn by A. de Neuville
• Fight of Archilles and Memnon (adapted from an Archaic Vase, Berlin)
• Pharos of Alexandria
• Hall in the Alexandrian Library

Acquisitions Editor: Roland S. Phelps
Technical Editor: Pat Mulholland-McCarty
Production: Katherine G. Brown
Book Design: Jaclyn J. Boone

# Contents

# Acknowledgments

I would like to take this opportunity to thank some of the many people and organizations who provided me with information and illustrative material during the preparation of this book:

Dennis Director of Director Technologies
Chuck Gilmore of Gilmore Systems
Ross Greenberg of Software Concepts Design
Jerry FitzGerald of Jerry FitzGerald & Associates
Pam Kane of Panda Systems
Al Leeds of The Washington Post Writers Group
Mike Riemer of FoundationWare

And special thanks go to Roland Phelps, Ron Powers, and the rest of the staff at TAB BOOKS for enthusiastically supporting this project.

# Introduction

Personal computer users have always had to protect their programs, files, and irreplaceable data from fire, hard drive crashes, poorly written software, and a multitude of other possible catastrophes. Recently, many PC users learned the hard way about a new means of losing data and even damaging equipment—the computer virus. The computer virus, and related programs such as Trojan horses, worms, and logic bombs, move silently from computer to computer under a shroud of secrecy and deceit. If they are not caught in time, these malicious programs can erase all the data off a hard drive, rearrange numbers in a spreadsheet file, or practically anything else a clever programmer can devise.

Personal computer users around the world have been hit recently by computer viruses and virus-type programs. In some cases, the programs were benign and simply displayed messages. But in the majority of cases, data was lost. Personal computer users have expressed outrage at these invisible programs that infect their computer systems. While most all brands of personal computers have been affected, the IBM-PC has been the hardest hit. Stories about infected computers pervade the most widely read newspapers and magazines, not only here in the United States, but overseas as well. Computer viruses have even been featured in an episode of *Star Trek: The Next Generation* and comic strips such as *Bloom County*, shown on the next page, and *Dick Tracy*.

# Introduction

## BLOOM COUNTY

©1989 Washington Post Writers Group reprinted with permission.

In this book, the mystery of computer viruses, Trojan horses, worms, and logic bombs is unraveled. You'll learn how these programs work, how to detect them, stop them, and recover from an attack by them. Specific steps that you can take to protect your personal computer system from infection are presented, along with information on available programs and DOS utilities you can use to inspect and protect your computer.

In Part I of this book, the subject of computer viruses and related virus-type programs is introduced. Many of the infamous viruses that have plagued personal computer users in the recent past are examined, as well as some viruses that have infected large computer systems and networks. You are taught how to protect your personal computer from infection or attack and how to recover from an attack.

In Part II, the computer virus problem and solutions are addressed specifically towards the IBM-PC and compatible family of computers. DOS is thoroughly examined, including common targets of viruses, such as the boot sector and FAT. Many commercial, shareware, and freeware anti-viral programs are covered, and the disk accompanying this book contains some of the best shareware and public domain anti-viral programs around. Finally, comprehensive anti-viral operating strategy is presented that allows you the freedom to use your computer as you like and still maintain an element of protection against viruses, Trojans, and worms.

I hope you find the book informative and useful. Should you notice any errors or omissions, please contact me through TAB BOOKS, Inc. The address is on the copyright page.

# PART I

# Introducing
# the Computer Virus

Part I introduces computer viruses, related programs, and what to do about them. Trojan horse
programs, worms, logic bombs and many well
known, as well as recently discovered viruses are
covered in Chapter 1. Chapter 2 concentrates on the
personal computer aspects of computer viruses and
related programs. Paths of infection are explained
and defensive computing strategies are developed.
Chapter 2 also covers proper procedures for
eradicating a malicious program and restoring
normal operations if your personal computer is
infected.

# 1
# What is a Computer Virus?

# Introducing the Computer Virus

THE WORLD OF PERSONAL COMPUTING IS TEEMING with talk of computer viruses. Everyone seems to have a story to tell, but the sure facts about viruses are still difficult to find. As a personal computer (PC) user, you are probably interested in knowing exactly what a computer virus is; what it does; how to protect your system from being infected by one; and what to do if you suspect your system has been infected.

This chapter provides an introduction to the subject of computer viruses by differentiating them from other potentially harmful or malicious programs. After discussing these related programs, several well known computer viruses are discussed to demonstrate the capabilities of viral programs.

## LOGIC BOMBS, TROJANS, WORMS, AND VIRUSES

A *computer virus* is a computer program—no more and no less—that is potentially dangerous. Computer viruses do not "magically" appear; rather, they are planned and programmed by someone to accomplish a specific purpose. What makes computer viruses and related programs different from other computer programs, such as spreadsheets and word processors, is that they most often generate havoc and despair rather than increase productivity.

Computer viruses are often confused with similar types of programs known as Trojans and logic bombs. The best way to understand computer viruses is to understand Trojans and logic bombs. These two types of programs encompass much of what most computer viruses do, although you will learn that computer viruses are also very different.

A *logic bomb* is typically a very short program that is added to an existing program or, in some cases, a modification made to an existing program. It is called a logic bomb because it is set to "explode" when certain conditions are met. An apt analogy is pressure-triggered bombs that are sometimes hidden by terrorists in luggage stored in the unpressurized baggage compartments of airplanes. When the plane reaches high altitudes and the air pressure in the baggage compartment drops to the required level, the pressure bomb is triggered.

The computer equivalent to a pressure bomb is a logic bomb program hidden inside the complex computer code for an applications program, such as an accounting package. The logic bomb must be added to the application program by someone with

4

access to the computer system and the knowledge to alter the program. For this reason, most logic bombs are left by "insiders" who wish to hurt the organization serviced by the computer, such as a recently fired programmer. Once the programmer suspects that he might be fired, he writes a logic bomb and inserts it into the accounting software program. The logic bomb might be programmed to destroy all financial records on the computer system's disks on 01 January of the following year (see Fig. 1-1). Should the programmer not be fired, he can later remove the logic bomb.

Logic bombs do not affect personal computers to the degree that Trojans and viruses do because logic bombs are written for particular software programs running on particular hardware systems for a certain malignant reason. However, logic bombs have turned up in the PC world before.

One example is a word processing package that was distributed with a particular PC for free evaluation use for a limited time. Users who decided to make use of the word processor were expected to register with the company and pay a fee. Registered users then received a new copy of the program and related documentation. Unbeknownst to users of the word processor, a logic bomb was ticking away in all of the unregistered evaluation copies of the program. When the program was run after a particular date, well

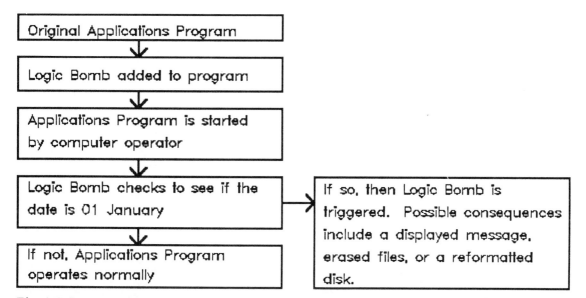

**Fig. 1-1.** *Diagram showing a trace of a possible logic bomb. When the date is 01 January, the logic bomb is triggered.*

after the evaluation period was over, the computer locked up and the word processor proceeded to delete all text files stored on the computer's disks.

Trojans are very similar to logic bombs in that when a Trojan is triggered, it can take control of a computer system and destroy data. Trojans get their name from the infamous Trojan horse of ancient times.

As you might recall from your classical studies, the Trojan horse was used by the Greeks in their battle against the fortress city of Troy during the Trojan War. The Trojan horse was a huge, hollow wooden structure in which several Greek soldiers hid. The horse was left outside Troy, and the Greeks feigned retreat. The citizens of Troy, believing that the long war was finally over, accepted the horse as a gift of surrender from the Greeks and brought it into the city. Later that night, as the citizens of Troy slept, the Greek soldiers exited from the horse and opened the city gates where they were met by the returning Greek armada. The Greeks

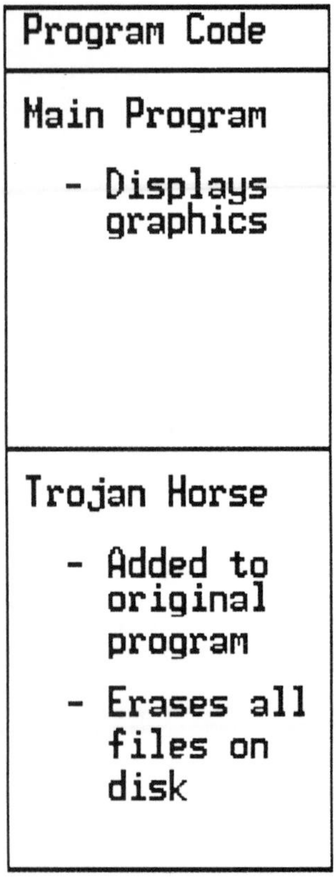

```
Program Code

Main Program

  - Displays
    graphics




Trojan Horse

  - Added to
    original
    program

  - Erases all
    files on
    disk
```

**Fig. 1-2.** A Trojan hidden in another program.

invaded the city, slaughtering and capturing many people, and thus winning the war.

A *Trojan*, in computer terms, is a program that appears to be legitimate while containing another program that is usually malicious (see Fig. 1-2). For example, a Trojan might be a computer game that also reformats the computer system's hard drive when played. Some Trojans are very sophisticated and have full featured front ends (the program the user believes is running) while others are very crude and don't do much except attempt to harm the system they are run on.

Trojans differ from logic bombs in that they are activated whenever they are run on the computer system. One famous Trojan is a graphics program that displays pretty images on the screen while it also corrupts data on the system's hard drive. Logic bombs and Trojans are nasty computer programs that can cause great anguish to PC users, but at least they are limited to the programs that contain them and the systems that these programs are run on—not so with computer viruses.

Computer virus programs are very similar to both Trojans and logic bombs, but much like their biological counterpart, computer viruses are capable of spreading to other programs on the computer system and even to other computer systems (see Fig. 1-3). Computer viruses can be thought of as independent, infectious logic bombs or Trojans.

Keep in mind that not all viruses, logic bombs, and Trojans are

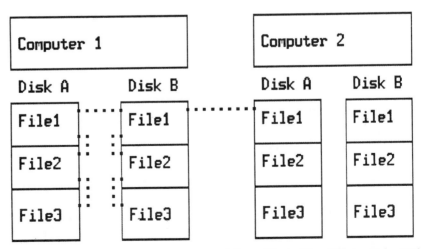

**Fig. 1-3.** *A computer virus can spread from file to file, disk to disk, and computer to computer.*

malicious programs. It is conceivable that a beneficial and productive program could be spread and/or triggered using these techniques. However, most all viruses, logic bombs, and Trojans are malicious and most computer users do not want unknown programs operating on their systems.

Another related type of computer program that is always malicious is the worm. A *worm* is a computer program designed to "slither" through a computer's memory and/or disks, altering any data that it encounters (see Fig. 1-4). Depending on the intentions of the worm's programmer, the worm might change all data to zeros or just subtly alter data by swapping individual bytes of stored information. The latter technique is more difficult to discover, and potentially much more dangerous. In many cases, programs continue to run even though some of the code has been altered. Any misspellings in text files might be assumed to be typographical errors. However, imagine the chaos that would occur if corrupted spreadsheet data were used for financial planning or if statistical data were altered.

## Memory before Worm

```
010101010101
010101010101
010101010101
010101010101
010101010101
010101010101
010101010101
010101010101
010101010101
```

## Memory after Worm

```
010101010100
010101010001
010101000101
010100010101
010001010101
000101010101
000001010101
010100010101
010101000101
```

**Fig. 1-4.** *A worm slithering through memory.*

8

To recap, computer virus programs are similar to logic bombs, Trojans, and worms. What makes a computer virus unique is its ability to automatically spread from program to program, file to file, and system to system. From a practical perspective, many people (including some within the computer community) group these similar programs under the generic heading of "computer virus." Using the definitions given in this section, you should be able to group a so-called "virus" into its appropriate category based on what it is and is not capable of doing.

Now that you have some theoretical background on what defines a computer virus, it is time to take a look at some of the better known viruses and related programs.

## INFAMOUS PC VIRUSES

There are several well publicized and well understood computer virus programs that serve as excellent examples of what virus-type programs are capable of doing, as well as giving you a little information about the history of the computer virus and related programs.

### The Pakistani-Brain Virus

One of the best known viruses in the IBM-PC world is the Pakistani, or Brain, virus. This virus gained national attention when it infected approximately one hundred PC compatible disks at the offices of *The Providence Journal-Bulletin* in early 1988. The Pakistani-Brain virus has also infected many other computer systems, including destroying patient records at a medical center and student's disks at several university computer centers.

The Pakistani-Brain virus replaces the original boot sector on infected disks. The original boot sector is moved to another location, and the remainder of the virus is stored on the disk in sectors flagged as unusable. The virus copies itself onto all bootable disks inserted into an infected computer. The virus is easy to detect because the volume label of an infected disk reads "BRAIN."

When triggered, the Pakistani-Brain virus corrupts information on the disk it has infected and displays a message that reads "Welcome to the Dungeon . . . Contact us for Vaccination" and goes on to list two names and the address for Brain Computer Services in Pakistan.

This virus was apparently written by one of the owners of Brain Computer Services in an attempt to protect software he had written from illegal copying, which is called *pirating*. The original virus apparently has been modified to be much more malicious and is thought to have been spread outside of Pakistan by foreigners who purchased infected software.

## The Scores Virus

The Scores virus is well known to most users of Apple Macintosh personal computer systems. Once infected with the virus, a Macintosh system will begin to operate erratically. The Scores virus is specifically targeted against two proprietary programs—identified as ERIC and VULT—developed by Electronic Data Systems (EDS). If a virus infects a Macintosh running one of these programs, the virus will cause the program to fail, or crash, shortly after the user executes the program.

## The MacMag-Peace Virus

Another well known Macintosh virus was commissioned by the editor of the Canadian Macintosh magazine, *MacMag*. This virus is also known as the Peace virus because on its trigger date of 02 March 1988—the first anniversary of the Mac II—the virus displayed a universal peace message. On the whole, the MacMag-Peace virus was rather benign. In fact, many infected Macintosh users never knew they were infected because they did not use their Macintosh computer on 02 March. After that date, the virus quietly erased itself.

The MacMag-Peace virus is different from other viruses for another reason: it is the first virus to infect commercially distributed software. *Freehand*, a graphics program from Aldus Corporation, was originally shipped infected with the virus.

One of Aldus' contract employees happened to run a game containing the virus on the Macintosh he was using for Aldus work. The virus subsequently infected disks containing files that were later sent to Aldus. At Aldus, the virus continued to spread, ultimately contaminating thousands of *Freehand* disks during duplication. The infected *Freehand* disks were then shipped to dealers. After the infection was discovered, Aldus recalled all the infected copies and replaced them with clean ones.

## The nVIR Virus

Yet another Macintosh virus, the nVIR is one of the most destructive viruses to infect the Macintosh to date. There are several different varieties of the nVIR virus resulting from the publication of its source code, which originated in West Germany in 1987. The basic nVIR virus can be easily spread and can thoroughly infect a Macintosh system in a few minutes. The nVIR virus causes frequent system crashes and loss of both data and programs; however, variations of the basic virus might have different effects.

## The Lehigh Virus

Another well known virus affecting IBM PCs is the Lehigh virus, so named because it first affected PCs at Lehigh University's microcomputer laboratories. The Lehigh virus infects the COMMAND.COM file, increasing its size by about 20 bytes. The creation date and time also change. After replicating itself four times, the virus destroys all system data on the infected disk.

## The Israeli-Friday 13th Virus

The Computation Center at the Hebrew University of Jerusalem was infected by a virus that affected IBM-PCs. This virus copied itself to all executable programs run on an infected machine. However, there was apparently an error, or *bug*, in the virus because an already infected program would be reinfected by the virus. Eventually, this caused programs to rapidly increase in size to the point where they would no longer fit into the PC's memory.

Once the virus was isolated, it was discovered that it was triggered to "go off" on a Friday the 13th. Many believe the intended target date was Friday, 13 May 1988—Israel's 40th anniversary. If the virus had been triggered, the infected programs would have been deleted from the disk. There are also several variations of this virus with different trigger dates.

## The Sunnyvale Slug

There is not a lot of information available about the Sunnyvale Slug virus. Apparently named after the California city, this virus infected the IBM-PCs at an anonymous California computer company. The virus displays messages such as "Greetings from Sunnyvale. Can you find me?" The virus is also malignant in that it modifies some computer commands to delete data rather than perform their intended function.

## Eggbeater

Eggbeater is not actually a computer virus. Rather, it is a well known Trojan that many people mistakenly identify as a virus. It is included here for that reason. Eggbeater is really a pronunciation of an IBM program named EGABTR, a utility that supposedly improves color graphics.

When run, the program does nothing to the computer's display screen, but in actuality it is deleting all the files on the system's disks. When finished deleting the files, the Trojan displays a message on the screen: "ARF, ARF! Gotcha!" Eggbeater is not a virus because it does not replicate itself. There are many Trojans similar to Eggbeater, and most involve some sort of animated graphics to draw the user's attention away from the system's very active disk drives.

IBM-PCs and Macintoshes are not the only personal computer systems that suffer with the plague of computer viruses. Because IBM-PCs and Macintoshes make up the majority of personal computers in use, most of the attention has been focused on these two systems. However, there are other types of PCs with virus problems. Many Commodore Amigas have been infected with a virus called SCA (for Swiss Cracking Association—creator of the virus). The Atari STs and Apple IIs are also targets of viruses and related programs.

Not all viruses occur on personal computers. In the next section, some other viruses that have affected larger computer systems are explained.

## OTHER VIRUSES

While personal computers may be the only daily contact most of us have with the world of computing, they are certainly not the only computers in use. Minicomputers and mainframes are used for the brunt of computer intensive tasks. While a virus on a PC might wipe out an individual's or small group's work, a virus on a mainframe can seriously disrupt very large groups of people, from a corporate environment or government to scientific research. This section takes a look at some of the better known viruses that affect large computing systems.

## The IBM Christmas Card

The IBM Christmas Card "virus" was not really a virus at all and did not infect a single computer system. However, it did have a devastating affect on IBM's international electronic mail (E-mail) network during December of 1987. The "virus program" was actually a sophisticated E-mail message that was generated in Europe. The message displayed a Christmas card on the receiver's screen while it also sent copies of itself to all E-mail addresses in the recipient's E-mail "address book." The message soon traversed the Atlantic ocean and entered other E-mail networks, including IBM's world-wide network. Soon after, the E-mail networks became clogged with copies of the Christmas card message flowing back and forth, effectively bringing them to a halt. It took from one to three days to purge the networks of the Christmas card message.

## The Cookie Virus

Educational computer networks have been infected by a virus modeled after the character Cookie Monster from *Sesame Street*. The virus interrupts user's work with a message reading "I want a cookie." The message repeats itself with increasing frequency until the user types in the word "cookie." Other versions of the program will delete user's text from the screen and append the phrase "Give me a cookie!" to the user's printed output.

## The USPA & IRA Virus

The USPA & IRA virus is actually a series of logic bombs combined with a virus. The USPA & IRA virus was placed in the computer system at the Texas headquarters of the United Services Planning Association Inc. and The Independent Research Agency for Life Insurance Inc. by a vengeful senior programmer who was fired in September of 1985. The programmer, Donald Burleson, was fired for using the company's computer facilities for private work. He also had been the firm's computer security officer. Therefore, when he illegally entered the computer center early one morning (presumably with a duplicate set of building keys) he knew that he would have little trouble disrupting the computer system.

Logging onto the computer with a system level password the company had neglected to change after firing him, Burleson was able to activate the malicious programs he had written three weeks earlier, before he was officially fired. In addition to activating his virus and logic bombs, he also deleted approximately 168,000 sales records and corrupted users' logon records.

Burleson's logic bombs included modifying file retrieval programs to power-down the computer system rather than retrieve records. Many other logic bombs, similar to this one, were found scattered throughout the computer's software programs. In addition, an actual virus was discovered. The virus program was designed to erase sections of memory, duplicate itself, and then execute again in thirty days.

Company officials decided to restart the computer system from scratch, purging all programs and data currently stored on the computer system. The operating system and application programs were reinstalled from factory original copies, and data, including the deleted sales records, was restored from backups predating the incident. The company then decided to sue Burleson.

Burleson was sued for $12,000 by USPA and IRA for the cost of restoring the computer system. In addition, a county district attorney decided to charge Burleson with a criminal felony charge under Texas' computer crime laws. Burleson was subsequently found guilty and sentenced to seven years of probation and ordered to pay $11,800 in reparations to USPA and IRA.

## The Internet Virus

Internet is an extensive nationwide computer network that links computer centers belonging to federal agencies, universities, research labs, and other government installations together, which allows them to send and receive programs, data, and E-mail. In all, over 250,000 individual computer systems are connected to the network. The Internet virus used the E-mail program Send.mail to overload the network and computer systems connected to it when it was activated in early November of 1988.

The virus program, which allegedly was written by a Cornell graduate student, took advantage of an undocumented flaw in the Send.mail program to take control of the network by replicating the virus and transmitting copies of itself to other computers. While the virus program did not attempt to delete any data, it quickly captured most, if not all, of the computer's processing capability and memory space to replicate and send itself to other sites.

The virus quickly spread across the country, invading other computer networks that were connected to Internet. When reports of infection began to surface, uninfected computer centers began to disconnect themselves from Internet. The infected sites had to be restarted after the virus was purged, a process taking up to several days. The FBI and Secret Service are investigating this incident under the Computer Fraud and Abuse Act of 1986.

## Core Wars

While Core Wars is not a virus per se, it does deserve mention in this section. Core Wars was a computer game developed by three programmers at Bell Laboratories over two decades ago. Core Wars is named after the core memory of these early computer systems. Played after hours on Bell's computers, Core Wars was a game in which self-replicating programs were pitted against one another. Each program attempted to destroy the other by overwriting its program code. Each program rapidly replicated itself in an attempt to overwrite its competitors and avoid being overwritten by them. After a certain amount of time, the computer was halted and the winner was the program with the greatest number of copies in the computer's memory.

Core Wars spread to other corporate and university computer laboratories. Core Wars was regarded as an amusing programming test by the participants to see who could write the best self-replicating program. However, as time advanced, and the isolated systems that Core Wars was played on were networked with other computer systems, the danger of a self-replicating program escaping from its host computer became all too real.

Many Core Wars participants decided to stop playing, but others continued, confident that their programming skills could keep their creations under control. In the early 1980s, the public became aware of Core Wars and many programmers gave it a try, the result was a massive increase in public knowledge and virus programs.

## SUMMARY

The Department of Defense is very concerned with the threat of a virus similar to the Internet virus entering computer systems associated with our country's defense. A special SWAT team of virus killers from around the nation has been formed. The Computer Emergency Response Team (CERT), is composed of computer experts from around the country who are ready to respond to any infection.

Computer viruses along with the simpler Trojans, logic bombs, and worms, are very dangerous programs. They are certainly not something the average personal computer user would like to have running clandestinely on his system. This chapter has provided you with background knowledge on computer viruses along with actual examples of their capabilities. The next chapter concentrates on how viruses and related programs are spread, along with what you can do to help protect your personal computer from infection.

# 2
# Understanding Computer Viruses

# Introducing the Computer Virus

I N ORDER TO PROTECT A PERSONAL COMPUTER FROM IN-
fection by a virus, it is very helpful to understand how viruses
work. In this chapter, the methods a virus can use to infect a
personal computer are examined. Trojan horses, logic bombs, and
worms are discussed, and based on the knowledge of how personal
computers are infected, some general guidelines for preventing
infection are given.

A key point to remember about these types of programs is that
they must be hidden from the operator of the personal computer
they are trying to affect. Not many users would knowingly execute
a program that does malicious damage to their computers. Because
of this, virus-type programs must be able to conceal themselves,
which they do in a variety of ways.

## HIDE AND SEEK

Typically, virus-type programs are hidden within the computer
executable code of an applications program. An *applications
program* is any program, with the exception of an operating system
program, that is used on the computer. Common examples are word
processors, spreadsheets, telecommunications packages, and
graphics programs. A virus-type program can infect any of these
programs.

A Trojan horse is the most common virus-type program that
affects an applications program. The most common types of
applications that a Trojan horse affects are games and graphics
programs.

Computer viruses also frequently infect applications programs.
An applications program infected by a computer virus is one of the
primary ways that a computer virus is spread. Each time the
application program is executed, the virus program also is executed.
The virus can then replicate and spread, and eventually trigger
some event, such as a message display or the formatting of a hard
drive. If the infected applications program is transferred to another computer, the other computer also will become infected (see Fig.
2-1).

Unlike a virus, a Trojan horse infected applications program
will not replicate. The Trojan horse program is usually custom
written for a particular applications program. Some applications
programs are even written around the Trojan horse program;
sometimes the applications programs are poorly written, non-
functional shells or they can be extensive, working programs. When

18

## Infected Applications Program

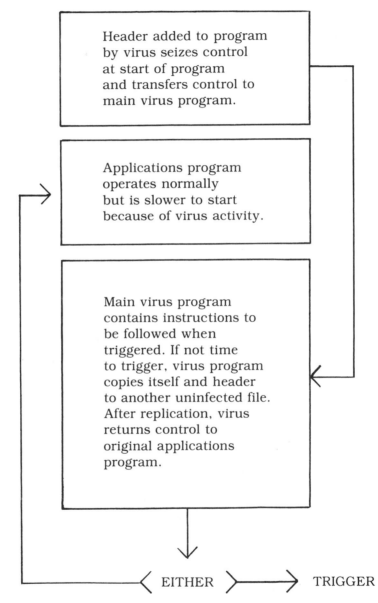

Header added to program
by virus seizes control
at start of program
and transfers control to
main virus program.

Applications program
operates normally
but is slower to start
because of virus activity.

Main virus program
contains instructions to
be followed when
triggered. If not time
to trigger, virus program
copies itself and header
to another uninfected file.
After replication, virus
returns control to
original applications
program.

EITHER     TRIGGER

**Fig. 2-1.** *When an infected application is run, the virus briefly seizes control of the computer to either trigger or replicate. If the conditions are not right to trigger, the virus replicates itself and returns control of the computer back to the applications program.*

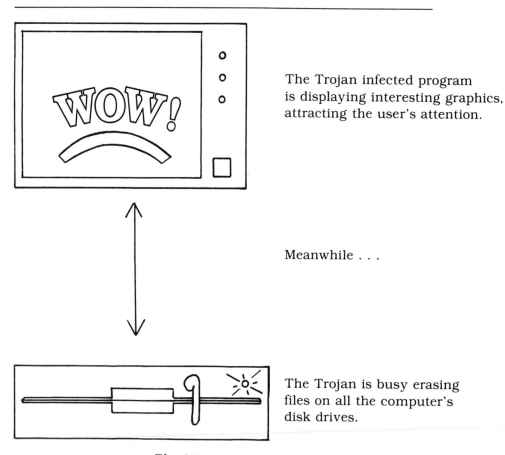

The Trojan infected program is displaying interesting graphics, attracting the user's attention.

Meanwhile . . .

The Trojan is busy erasing files on all the computer's disk drives.

**Fig. 2-2.** *A Trojan at work.*

an applications program containing a Trojan horse is executed, the Trojan horse program takes over and immediately carries out its instructions while the contaminated applications program continues to run (see Fig. 2-2).

The emphasis of this discussion thus far has been on applications programs. Applications programs are the programs that most personal computer operators use on a daily basis. After all, you bought your personal computer so that you could use applications programs. However, there is another classification of programs that all personal computers have—system programs.

*System programs* are the computer programs that your personal computer needs to operate. These programs are used to format disks, configure memory, keep track of stored files, decode keyboard signals, and a multitude of other tasks. Most often the system programs are packaged together in an integrated package known as the *operating system* (OS). Operating systems are also referred to as *Disk Operating Systems* (DOS).

Each type of personal computer has its own type of operating system. Perhaps the best known is Microsoft DOS (MS-DOS) for the IBM-PC and compatible machines. IBM also markets MS-DOS under its own label as PC-DOS. Other common operating systems include ProDOS for the Apple II, UNIX, CP/M, and OS/9.

Most personal computer users are not very familiar with the inner workings of the operating system on their computer. Other than when formatting disks and copying files, many users are never even aware they are using the operating system. However, it is important to have a good understanding of your computer's operating system if you are going to successfully protect it from computer viruses.

In order to keep the virus-type programs as short as possible to avoid detection, many virus-type programs make use of the operating system to perform some of their nasty handiwork. There are also many computer viruses that directly infect operating system programs. The next chapter discusses the IBM-PC operating system in detail.

## PATH OF INFECTION

Now that you know how virus-type programs can affect your personal computer, the next step is to look at common ways that virus-type programs and/or the programs that contain them are transferred from their originator's computer to other personal computer systems. Computer programs can be transferred in a variety of ways. The most common means of program distribution is via floppy disks. Other methods of transferring computer programs include different types of media, such as CD-ROM and tape, as well as telecommunications (see Fig. 2-3).

When you purchase a computer program, it comes stored on a floppy disk. The 5¼-inch and 3½-inch size disks are the most common. After receiving a computer program on a floppy disk, most users either make working copies of the program on other floppy disks or copy the program from a floppy disk to their hard drive. A hard drive can contain thousands of programs, data, and other files.

## Disk Based

- User to user
- Company to user
- Author to user

## Telecommunications

- Bulletin board systems
- Information services
- Uploading and downloading
- Telephone lines
- Networks
- Electronic mail
- File transfers

**Fig. 2-3.** *Some of the common means of transferring computer files.*

In the case of floppy disk transfers, a virus can get into a personal computer in one of two ways: 1) via a copied program or file from the disk or 2) through the virus' own replication process. Should you run a virus infected program stored on a floppy disk, it is possible for the virus to copy itself to other programs stored on other disks that are attached to the computer.

A Trojan horse program will not replicate; however, if triggered, the Trojan can affect the entire computer system—not just the disk that the program is stored on. Each copy of the Trojan laced program also will contain the Trojan horse program. A worm program contained on a floppy disk based program can work its way into memory, and it can affect information currently in memory that might be saved later on disk.

In some cases, if the operating system files stored on the disk are infected with a virus-type program, it is possible for the Trojan to trigger or the virus to replicate without the user knowingly having executed any of the programs stored on the disk. This happens because many operating system programs are utilized by the computer without the knowledge of the average user.

Sources of floppy disks infected with virus-type programs include just about any place you get software. Be especially wary if you do not know the source of the disk you are putting into your computer's disk drive. It is even possible for commercial, "shrink wrapped," software packages to be infected as was demonstrated by the Aldus *Freehand* incident. Many user's groups have program libraries containing tens of thousands of programs for particular personal computers. Make sure you trust the source of the disks you get through them.

Now is a good time to bring up the discussion about the main types of software—commercial, shareware, freeware, and public domain. *Commercial software* is the computer programs you purchase from established companies, such as Microsoft and Borland. An easy way to identify commercial software is: 1) by the price of the package, which is usually expensive; 2) the physical quality of the documentation (professionally printed and bound); and 3) the license agreement that comes with it. If the license agreement prohibits copying the program and is very legal-looking, then the accompanying software programs are probably classified as commercial.

You should be very wary of any copies of commercial software that you might run across. Distributing copies of commercial software packages is in most cases very illegal, so the person you are getting it from is already involved in a shady practice known as pirating (copying and distributing commercial programs). It is possible that the programs might have been altered to include a Trojan horse or worm program, or that the disks are infected with a virus. Think about it; the person that copied these disks probably has hundreds of other illegal copies of commercial software packages that have been used at least once on his computer system. It is not unlikely that he might have picked up, even without his knowledge, a virus from one of them. The bottom line is do not put disks containing copies of commercial software in your disk drives unless you can clearly trace the generations of copies back to the original factory disks.

*Shareware* is similar to commercial software in many ways. Under the shareware system, users are allowed to copy, distribute, and use shareware programs without paying for them up front. Should the program prove useful, the user is expected to pay the author of the program a fee that is usually specified in the documentation.

Because shareware programs can be legally distributed by persons other than the author, they can have the same problems as illegal commercial software copying in that they can be infected by virus-type programs somewhere in the distribution path. Most copies of shareware programs are perfectly clean; however, always be careful. If you have any doubts about a shareware program that you receive, you can contact the author for a clean copy (many will charge a nominal fee for disk and shipping costs). Most shareware authors are very aware of the virus problem, and take steps to ensure that their copies are not infected.

*Freeware* is very similar to shareware with the exception that there is no fee for the software. The author of the program allows the program to be distributed and used without receiving any compensation. The same cautions regarding shareware also apply to freeware.

Public domain software also has no fee attached to it. *Public domain software* is just that, software in the public domain. The author of the program claims no copyrights to the software; users are free to do what they want with the programs. The authors of public domain software are sometimes difficult to locate. There are many fine public domain programs available for a variety of personal computers; however, there is a lot of junk as well.

Because the programs are in the public domain, users are free to play with the program, often rewriting parts of it. The result is that there can be many different versions of the same program. Because there is usually no way to know if you have a clean copy of the program other than to run it, you should only use public domain programs that are obtained from reliable sources and used by others without trouble.

Thus far, the discussion on distributing programs has been limited to the floppy disk, and the same controls already discussed also apply to other forms of media. Another means of distributing programs is telecommunications. *Telecommunications* is the transfer of data between separate computer systems without the need for exchange of physical media. In the personal computer world, telecommunications usually refers to connecting your computer to remote computer systems over the telephone with a modem.

Telecommunications is a popular means of transferring programs between personal computers. Personal computers equipped with modems can connect to remote computers which store many programs and other files that can be downloaded by its users.

There are two classes of remote computer systems—bulletin boards and information services. *Bulletin boards* are usually personal computers that are connected to the telephone service via a modem. Other personal computer users who connect to the bulletin board can upload and download programs and other files and leave messages for other users. *Information services* are large remote computer sites, usually using mainframes and other large computer systems, that can handle thousands of simultaneous users that connect over the telephone lines. Information services have hundreds of thousands of programs and other files available for downloading, feature an extensive electronic mail system, and have large databases available for searching.

*Bulletin boards* are usually run by individuals or user's groups. There are thousands of bulletin board systems spread across the nation and the world. The quality of a bulletin board depends almost entirely on the system operator (SYSOP) that manages it. Many shareware, freeware, and public domain programs are available for downloading from the bulletin board. In addition, users can upload their own programs to the bulletin board for other users to download.

Typically, there is no fee for using a bulletin board other than the long distance telephone charges when you call it. At most, approximately ten users can be connected simultaneously. From the perspective of protecting your system from virus-type programs, you should approach bulletin boards with care. Contact the system operator to see if he screens uploaded files for Trojans, worms, or viruses. If not, it is probably best not to download any programs from that bulletin board.

Information services are run by corporations. Three of the biggest information services are CompuServe, Genie, and The Source. There are usually local telephone access numbers near major cities in the United States, so a toll call is usually not necessary to access them. However, information services do charge an access fee for their use.

Information services also contain a large number of shareware, freeware, and public domain programs. It is much safer to download these programs from an information service than an average bulletin board because the information service screens all uploads. There are one or two cases where people downloaded programs containing virus-like programs from an information service, but the problem was quickly discovered and the offending programs removed.

Regardless of whether you download a program from a bulletin board or an information service, apply the same precautions that you would with a floppy disk based program. If you save the downloaded program to a clean disk and the program itself is clean, you should not have any problems. If the program does contain a virus-type program, your system is still not in danger of infection unless you execute the program, triggering the virus-type program.

The bottom line is to make sure you obtain the programs you

run on your computer from the most reliable source possible. That is the best way to make sure you do not get a virus-type program in your computer. Commercial or shareware software ordered directly from the company or author is the safest way to obtain software (other than writing it yourself). Next comes legal copies of noncommercial software obtained from a trusted person who has been using the software without incident for several months. Finally, software downloaded from information services and reputable bulletin boards will probably be fine. Avoid, at all costs, illegal copies of commercial software and other programs from unknown sources.

## DEFENSIVE ACTION

Even assuming that you follow all of the suggestions in the previous section, it is still possible, however remote, for your personal computer to get infected. This section discusses numerous useful ways to minimize the damage that a Trojan horse, worm, logic bomb, or computer virus can do your computer system.

The best advice is to know your system. For example:

- Know what files are stored on your hard drive
- Know the type and version of the operating system you are using
- Observe your computer in action. How long does it normally take to start up? How long does it take to load a particular program and respond to commands?
- Find out how much free disk space you have and monitor it

In general, get to know your computer as best you can. That way, you will know when it starts to act strangely—even minute changes. Like cancer, if you observe a problem in its early stages, it is much easier to fix.

**Backup your programs and data** The very first thing you should do to defend yourself against a future attack from a virus-type program is to backup your programs and data. This way, should your hard drive be reformatted or your floppy disks corrupted, you can still recover with little trouble. There are many different methods of backing up. For floppy disks, simply make duplicate copies. In the case of a hard drive, use floppy disks, tape, or some other form of backup. Make regular backups and keep complete backups going back approximately six months. That way, should you get infected by a virus and not notice it for a few months, you can restore it from an uninfected backup. Part II of this book discusses backup procedures in more detail for the IBM-PC and compatibles.

**Write-protect the original disks**    The next thing you should do is to write-protect all your original factory master disks. This will prevent the computer from every storing information on them. To write-protect a 5¼-inch disk, cover the write-protect notch with a write-protect tab. With 3½-inch disks, open the sliding tab so that you can see through the tiny square opening. Never use master copies for everyday work; only use them for making copies.

If you boot your computer from floppy disks, make a clean boot disk with the write-protected factory master operating system disks. Then write-protect the new boot disk also. Only use that boot disk to boot the system. Do not boot the computer with another floppy disk. This will eliminate the possibility of your booting from a disk with an infected operating system.

If you have a computer that boots off the hard drive, do not boot off of a floppy disk unless you are sure it is clean. The best way to do this is to configure the disk yourself using write-protected factory master copies of the operating system. Then when you install the operating system on your hard drive, make sure you use the write-protected factory master copies. The same rationales in the previous paragraph apply here.

**Reboot the computer between running programs, especially games**    This will, depending on the system, reset the computer's memory and reload any memory resident operating system programs from the disk. Otherwise, a virus or worm might remain in memory, ready to attack the next program or data loaded into memory. Also, reboot before and after formatting disks for an extra measure of safety.

**Monitor the usage of your computer**    If other people use your computer, make sure they do not use any disks that you have not already checked out. Make sure the users of your computer understand the virus problem and the steps you have taken to protect the computer.

Be very careful when running new software for the first time. Make sure there are no other disks in the drives. Run the program from floppy disks if at all possible. This way, should the program have a Trojan or virus, it might not spread beyond the disk it is stored on.

**Always monitor your computer system carefully when running new software**    Read the documentation thoroughly before starting the program. Make sure there are no extra files on the disk that do not belong there. Some software documentation lists the names and sizes of all the files included in the package. If so, compare the files on your disk to the ones listed. If they do not match, do not run the program.

**If a program comes without any documentation, be extremely wary of it**    Look for a help or text file on the disk. If there is not one, and you cannot locate the name and address of the author, distributor, or company, do not run the program. Any decent program will have at least minimal documentation, and the author or company will be prominently displayed somewhere in the files.

A big clue to whether a program is really what it says is the size of the program. If you have what is supposed to be a full featured word processor, and the program is only 5,000 or so bytes long, something is very wrong. Also, look at the file creation date. If it is far in the past or future, something might be wrong. Should you decide to run these programs, be very cautious.

**Keep track of the creation date and size of files on your disk**    This is one of the more tedious tasks you can perform to protect your system. Should the size and/or date of an executable file change, it is possible that it has been infected. You can also compare files with their equivalent on the write-protected master copies of your programs.

If you are using your computer for business, there are a few additional precautions that you might want to take. At the risk of taking the ''personal'' out of personal computers, you can simply eliminate the use of public domain, freeware, and all but very well known shareware programs. In addition, you can simply never download programs from bulletin boards. Another good rule is to never play computer games on your work computer. Just stick with several commercial packages to be as safe as possible.

## ON THE OFFENSIVE

OK, you're sure you have been infected by a virus, or that a Trojan horse has been triggered on your personal computer. What now? The first thing you should do is make sure that what you think is the handiwork of a virus-type program is not actually a buggy program, malfunctioning hardware, or user error. Sometimes it is very obvious that you have been hit by a virus-type program—if a message to that effect pops up on your screen, for example. Other times, it can be more subtle.

If, after rationally examining the situation, you are still sure you have been hit, it is time to plan a recovery strategy.

**Try to pinpoint exactly when the virus, Trojan, or worm entered your computer**    For example, has your computer started acting strangely since you played that new game you downloaded Friday night? If so, make sure you do a restore using data backed up previous to the attack. If you cannot determine when the computer was infected, use the oldest backups you have for safety's sake.

**The next step is to determine the extent of the damage**    Are all the drives infected? Just the floppy disk containing the program? What floppy disks did you put into the computer since the time you believe it was infected? Be very liberal about all of the answers. It is much better to fix too much than too little. Unless you're an experienced computer user, do not plan on trying to repair the infected disks; just reformat them and recopy clean copies of the software and files back onto them.

Most viruses only infect executable programs, not text or other nonexecutable files. It might be possible to copy the nonexecutable files off the infected disk and reuse them. Use a word processor or text editor to check the files for damage. If you're dealing with a worm or other data altering program, don't try to reuse anything.

**Turn your computer off for at least five minutes, then reboot using a clean, write-protected copy of your operating system**    Now reformat all affected disks. Be careful not to run any programs on any of the infected disks, and make sure all disks you put in the drives are write-protected. Once the disks are formatted, turn the computer off again for at least five minutes before booting up again. Now you can restore files to the reformatted disks using write-protected originals.

If you know how you have been infected, notify the source of the program. And be sure never to use that program again. A computer virus or Trojan attack can be nerve-racking, especially if you use your computer for business. The best defense against virus-type programs is thorough backups. That way, should you get attacked, you can restore back to before the attack.

## SUMMARY

This chapter has covered in a non-hardware specific manner how computer viruses, Trojan horse programs, worms, and logic bombs work. The various ways infected disks and programs are distributed was discussed. Numerous guidelines for protecting your personal computer from attack or infection were presented, along with information on how to ride out and recover from an assault by a malicious program.

This concludes Part I. Part II is specific to the IBM-PC and compatibles and provides more detailed information for users of this type of personal computer.

# PART II

# Computer Viruses
## and the IBM-PC

Part II of this book focuses on computer viruses and their effect on the IBM-PC and compatibles. Chapter 3 introduces DOS, which is the operating system used by the IBM-PC. Floppy and hard disks are covered, and prime virus targets, such as the boot sector and FAT are explained. Numerous DOS utilities are discussed that can be used to monitor your IBM-PC. In Chapter 4, anti-viral programs, utilities, and hardware are covered. Chapter 5 ties all the information together with the goal of virus-proofing your PC.

# 3
# The IBM-PC
# vs
# Malicious Programs

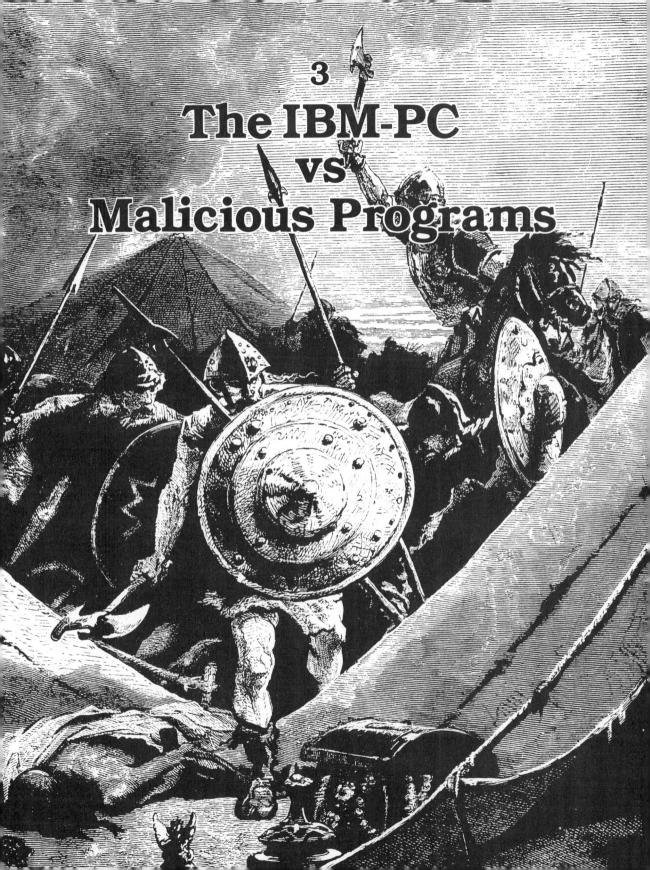

**D**UE TO THEIR TREMENDOUS POPULARITY, IBM-PC AND compatible computers are frequently the target of computer virus, Trojan horse, and worm programs. Fortunately for users of the IBM-PC, these computers have a very open architecture—both in hardware and software. Just as you can open up an IBM-PC's case and plug in expansion cards or play with jumpers and dip switches, you can use software to explore the computer's memory and disk storage.

This chapter takes a look at the problem of computer virus, Trojan, and worm programs from the perspective of the IBM-PC. First, the areas that are most affected by virus-type programs —memory and disk storage—are explored. Following that is a discussion of the IBM-PC's operating system software. There are several programs included with PC-DOS that can be used to detect, and even recover from, an attack by a computer virus-type program. This chapter ends with a look at the current computer virus crisis from the perspective of a user of an IBM-PC.

Much of the information contained in this chapter can be applied to general IBM-PC computing; it is not specific for computer virus-type programs. However, only the information relevant to understanding the effects of virus-type programs has been included. If you are interested in learning more about the IBM-PC, you are encouraged to refer to a book written specifically on that topic.

## THE IBM-PC AND IBM-PC COMPATIBLES

In order to make use of the information contained in this part of the book, you must be using an IBM-PC or compatible personal computer. If you are sure that your computer is an IBM-PC or compatible, you can skip this section. However, if you are not sure, then this section helps you find out.

A sure way to determine whether you have an IBM-PC compatible personal computer is by the type of operating system. IBM-PCs use the MS-DOS and PC-DOS disk operating systems. This will guarantee that your computer can run most, if not all, of the software written for the IBM-PC. However, there are many personal computers in existence that can use the IBM-PC operating system but are not compatible on a hardware level with an IBM-PC.

A hardware level compatible IBM-PC contains an Intel 8086, 8088, 80186, 80286, or 80386 microprocessor. There are a few microprocessors, such as the NEC V-20 and V-30, that are compatible with some of the Intel microprocessors. Most all IBM-PC compatibles also contain between three and ten expansion slots for add-on circuit boards.

If your personal computer uses PC-DOS or MS-DOS, has an Intel or compatible microprocessor, and has expansion slots, it is most likely compatible with the IBM-PC. You can be extra certain by running MS-DOS software such as the Microsoft Flight Simulator. If your system passes all these tests, it is compatible enough with the IBM-PC to make use of the information in this part of the book.

## PC, XT, AT, OR 386

Not only is it important to know that you have an IBM-PC compatible computer, but also where it fits in the line of IBM-PC personal computers. The first IBM-PC is known as the PC. It has a small power supply, limited memory expansion capability, no hard drive, and uses an Intel 8088 microprocessor. The PC/XT is an improvement on the PC. It has a larger power supply, more memory, a hard drive, and also contains the Intel 8088. The AT is a step up from the XT. The AT has an Intel 80286 microprocessor and includes CMOS RAM. The 386 refers to any personal computer based on the Intel 80386 microprocessor; in most all other respects, it is very similar to an AT.

## THE IBM-PC'S MEMORY

The internal memory architecture used in personal computers differs from one model to another. Fortunately, all IBM-PC compatibles that are run under PC-DOS or MS-DOS have roughly the same internal memory architecture. Thus, the concepts discussed in this section will apply to all types of IBM-PC compatibles.

There are two types of physical memory: RAM and ROM. RAM stands for *Random Access Memory*, and ROM stands for *Read Only Memory*. The key difference between these types of memory is that RAM can be both written to and read from, while ROM can only be read from once initially "burned in." RAM is the memory where programs and data are stored and where information that is stored is lost when the computer's power is turned off. ROM, as the definition implies, contains programs and data that do not change and retains the information stored in it even when the computer's power is turned off.

There is much more to the IBM-PC's internal memory architecture than is contained in the following paragraphs; however, this explanation is adequate for understanding how virus-type programs can affect memory.

## RAM

There are also several types of RAM. The most common is conventional memory. *Conventional memory* includes the first 640 kilobytes, or K, of RAM. A kilobyte is 1024 bytes, and a byte is composed of eight bits. A single character is represented inside the computer by a unique combination of eight bits, or one byte. RAM above the conventional memory limit of 640K is either extended or expanded memory.

*Extended memory* is found only on IBM-PCs using the Intel 80286 or higher microprocessors. For example, the 80286 can address up to 16 megabytes of RAM, the portion above 640K referred to as extended memory. Expanded memory can be found on all types of IBM-PC compatibles.

*Expanded memory* is simply an extension of conventional memory, rather than a continuation as with extended memory. The computer thinks it has only conventional memory, but through clever switching techniques, banks of memory can be exchanged into conventional memory. This gives the ability to have megabytes of RAM on IBM-PC compatibles that do not support extended memory.

Yet another type of RAM is CMOS. *CMOS* is a type of RAM that is battery backed so that it does not lose the information stored in it when the computer is turned off. It is usually found in IBM-PC compatibles with 80286 or higher microprocessors and is used to store configuration information about the computer system.

## ROM

The main ROM contained in an IBM-PC compatible computer system is the ROM-BIOS. BIOS stands for *Basic Input Output System* and is part of the IBM-PC's operating system. The BIOS is responsible for handling the hardware input and output requests for the computer system. The remainder of the operating system is loaded into RAM and is stored on disk. Other ROM in the IBM-PC can be found on graphics cards and on hard drive controller cards. Unchanging programs necessary to use these cards are stored there.

## DISK DRIVES

There are two main types of disk drives currently in use today: floppy disks and hard drives. Most IBM-PCs today have one or two floppy disks and a hard drive for online storage. This section explores several aspects of both floppy and hard drives that are relevant to understanding how virus-type programs can affect them.

## Floppy Disks

In the IBM-PC world of computing, floppy disks come in two sizes, 5¼-inch and 3½-inch (see Figs. 3-1 and 3-2). Through a variety of storage techniques that are covered later, the 5¼-inch disks can store 160K, 180K, 320K, 360K, and 1,200K (1.2Mb) of information. The 3½-inch disks can store either 720K or 1,440K (1.44Mb).

Physically, a floppy disk consists of a circular piece of plastic film that is coated with a magnetically sensitive iron-oxide coating.

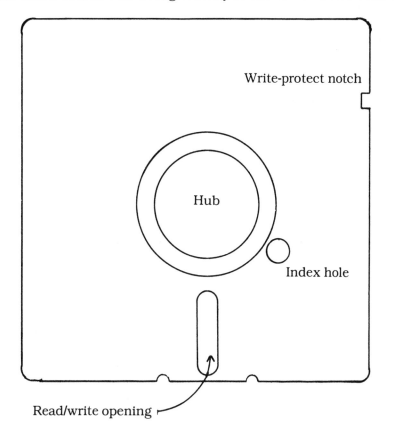

Write-protect notch

Hub

Index hole

Read/write opening

5.25"

**Fig. 3-1.** *A diagram of a 5¼-inch floppy disk.*

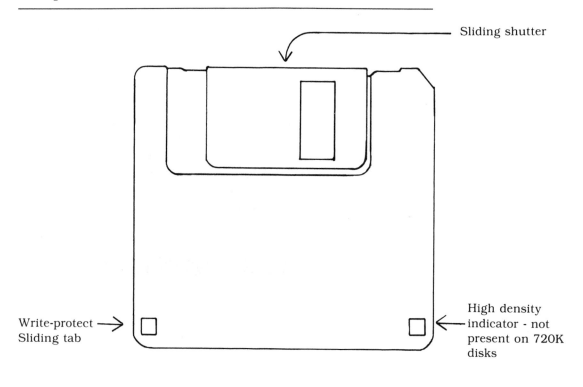

**Fig. 3-2.** A diagram of a 3½-inch disk.

The circular film is enclosed within a protective jacket. The 5¼-inch disk has a flexible plastic jacket while the 3½-inch disk has a rigid plastic jacket.

There is a read/write opening cut into the jacket so that the head of the disk drive can read and write to the iron-oxide coating. In 3½-inch disks, the read/write opening is covered by a spring loaded shutter. In the center of the disk is the hub. The *hub* is where the disk drive's motor mechanism grasps the mylar film so that it can be rotated.

The final important detail about floppy disks is the write-protect mechanism. The disk drive will not write to a disk that has its write-protect mechanism activated. On 5¼-inch disks, the write-protect mechanism consists of a small cutout on the side of the jacket. If the cutout is open, the disk is write enabled and the drive will be able to write information to the disk. To write-protect the disk, the cutout is covered with a sticky, tape-like tab.

The 3½-inch disk has a slightly different write-protect mechanism. In one corner of the 3½-inch disk's rigid jacket is a small square cutout with a built-in sliding tab. If the sliding tab is closed so that you cannot see through the cutout, the disk is write enabled. To write-protect the disk, slide the tab so that the cutout is open. Note that on some 3½-inch disks there are two square cutouts. One of the cutouts is the write-protect mechanism and the other is used to indicate to the disk drive that the disk is a high density (1.44Mb) disk. The 720K 3½-inch disks, obviously, have one one cutout.

A new disk, regardless of size, must be formatted before any information can be stored on it. During the formatting process, the surface(s) of the disk is organized into concentric tracks. Each track also is divided into sectors (see Fig. 3-3). A disk can have either one or two sides formatted; one formatted side is called single-sided, and two formatted sides is called double-sided. The number of tracks and sectors per track can also vary. The standard 360K disk is double-sided and has 40 tracks with 9 sectors per track. Each sector holds 512 bytes of information, so that's 4,608 bytes per track, 184,320 bytes per side, and 368,640 bytes per disk.

When the disk is formatted, certain control information is written to the disk. The very first sector of the disk is the Boot Sector. The boot sector is followed by the File Allocation Table (FAT). The boot sector contains information about the FAT and the format of the disk. In addition, if the disk has been formatted as a boot disk (a disk that contains operating system files necessary to load DOS into the computer), the boot sector includes DOS information as well as the names of the system files stored on the disk.

The FAT is a record keeping area where DOS keeps track of where information is located on the disk. There is an entry in the FAT for each location on the disk that can store data. When information is written to the disk, the FAT is updated to reflect where the information is stored. Each entry indicates the next entry where more of the information is stored or if the current entry is the last entry. Because the FAT is vital to finding stored information on the disk, DOS usually maintains two copies. If one becomes corrupted, the other can be referenced.

Following the FAT(s) is the Root Directory. The root directory is where the names of the files (commonly called filenames) contained in the root directory are listed. Under DOS, a filename can have up to eight characters, a period, and a three character

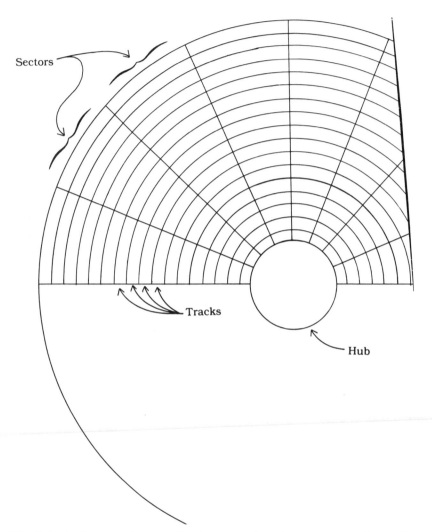

**Fig. 3-3.** *A diagram showing the tracks and sectors on the surface of the disk.*

extension (i.e. PROGRAM.EXE). The root directory also contains the names of other subdirectories contained on the disk. The root directory can contain from 64 to 224 filename or subdirectory entries, depending on the type of disk.

## Hard Disks

Hard disks are also called *fixed disks*, *rigid disks*, and *winchester drives*. A hard drive is a high capacity storage device that is similar to floppy disks in many ways. A typical hard drive used on an IBM-PC contains between 20 and 150 megabytes of storage space. Having this much storage space requires a more complicated DOS management system.

Physically, a hard drive consists of several rigid platters and double the number of read/write heads (one for each side of each platter) encased in a sealed box. Because hard drives store so much information, their magnetic surfaces are of very high quality. In addition, they rotate at a much higher speed than floppy disks (300 rpm vs 3,600 rpm).

Formatting a hard drive requires three separate steps.

1) First comes the *low-level* format. This is done using software supplied with the disk or contained in ROM on the hard drive controller card. The low-level format divides the disk into cylinders (the hard drive equivalent of tracks) and sectors. A typical hard drive has approximately 300 cylinders and 17 sectors per cylinder. The number of platters, the number of cylinders per platter, and the number of sectors per cylinder determine the total storage space available on the drive.

2) The next step is *partitioning* which is done using DOS' FDISK program. FDISK is used to divide the disk into partitions. Most IBM-PC users elect to use the entire hard drive as a PC-DOS disk, but it is possible to use the same hard drive with multiple operating systems, such as Xenix and CP/M-86. With FDISK, the portions of the hard drive that will be available to PC-DOS are defined. FDISK also can be used to view currently defined partition information (see Fig. 3-4).

A hard drive can be divided into one or more DOS partitions, and each partition will be assigned a logical drive designation beginning with the letter C. In older versions of DOS, the maximum partition size was 32 megabytes, so drives with larger capacities had to be partitioned into smaller logical drives. Current versions of DOS support single partitions in excess of 32 megabytes.

FDISK records all this information in the Master Boot Record (MBR). The MBR indicates where the operating system begins on the disk, how big it is, and whether it is currently active. The MBR is stored on the very first sector of the disk.

3) After partitioning the disk, a *high-level* format is done using the DOS FORMAT command, the same program used to format a floppy disk. FORMAT once again creates a DOS Boot Sector and a FAT for each DOS partition. The primary partition, usually on

```
Display Partition Information

Current Fixed Disk Drive: 1

Partition Status    Type  Start  End Size
  C: 1         A   PRI DOS     0  511  512
     2             EXT DOS   512 1022  511


Total disk space is 1023 cylinders.


The Extended DOS partition contains
logical DOS drives. Do you want to
display logical drive information?   [Y]


Press ESC to return to FDISK Options
```

**Fig. 3-4.** *Partition information about my hard drives obtained with FDISK.*

the boot drive C, contains the DOS system files necessary to boot the computer. Each partition also has a root directory, as with floppy disks.

## DOS

The Disk Operating System (DOS) has been referred to throughout this chapter. DOS is the program, or programs, that supervises and directs the operation of the computer. The standard DOS that has been mentioned is PC-DOS which is basically the same as MS-DOS. Microsoft developed the DOS for the IBM-PC when it was first released. IBM licensed DOS from Microsoft and sold it as PC-DOS. Microsoft also sells the DOS as MS-DOS. There are many MS-DOS packages that have been customized for particular computers. For example, there is a MS-DOS for Zenith computers. These customized versions do not differ greatly from the standard PC-DOS. In this book PC-DOS, MS-DOS, and DOS are used interchangeably and DOS is used to refer to any disk operating system.

Part of DOS, the BIOS, is stored in ROM in the computer. The remainder of DOS comes stored on disks. There are three main files that are required to be present for DOS to operate. These are IBMBIO.COM, IBMDOS.COM, and COMMAND.COM on the PC-DOS operating system. The same files are called IO.SYS, MSDOS.SYS, and COMMAND.COM on the MS-DOS operating system. IBM-BIO.COM, and its MS-DOS equivalent IO.SYS, is an extension of the ROM BIOS and contains routines for controlling and communicating with peripherals. IBMDOS.COM and MSDOS.SYS contains file handling routines for both disks and other peripherals.

COMMAND.COM is the Command Processor. It contains many routines for processing commands entered by the computer's user. It is COMMAND.COM that presents the C> prompt. There are two parts to COMMAND.COM, one is memory resident and the other is transient. The memory resident portion always remains in memory, and the transient portion is loaded into memory but is removed if the memory space is needed by another program. The transient portion contains several of the common DOS commands such as DIR and COPY.

If you look at the root directory of a DOS boot disk, you can see COMMAND.COM, but not the other two files. The other two files are hidden files. A file can have up to four attributes: *system, hidden, read-only*, and *archive*. A file with the hidden attribute set will not show up on any directory listings. Likewise, a file with the read-only attribute set cannot be altered by DOS.

The DOS package also includes many programs that are very helpful for managing files under DOS. Several that can be of help in monitoring the PC to prevent or minimize damage caused by a virus-type program are ATTRIB, BACKUP, CHKDSK, COMP, DISKCOMP, FDISK, FORMAT, RESTORE, and SYS. In the following sections, we'll examine each of these utilities.

## ATTRIB

ATTRIB is used to set or reset the read-only attribute; it can also be used to display the current setting. This can come in very handy when we want to protect a file from being written over, either accidently or by a malicious program. To make a file read-only, type

ATTRIB +R *<filename.ext>*

To remove the read-only attribute from a file, type

    ATTRIB − R <*filename.ext*>

Finally, to view the current setting of the read-only attribute, type

    ATTRIB <*filename.ext*>

## BACKUP and RESTORE

As mentioned earlier, the best defense against an attack by a virus-type program is backups. While floppy disks can be easily copied, backing up a hard drive can be a chore. To help with this task, DOS includes a rudimentary backup and restoration system. BACKUP is used to copy the files to floppy disks and RESTORE is used to get them back.

Because BACKUP and RESTORE involve many options, see your DOS manual for more information.

## CHKDSK

CHKDSK is one of the most valuable DOS utilities. CHKDSK analyzes the FAT, directories, and files on a disk and produces a disk and memory status report. CHKDSK also can be used to fix simple errors in the directory or FAT. To run CHKDSK, type

    CHKDSK <C:> /F/V

The /F is used when you want CHKDSK to fix any errors it finds, and the /V option causes CHKDSK to display all files and their paths.

The status report is a good way to keep track of what is going on in your computer. It reports the total amount of space on the disk, the number and space consumed by hidden files and regular files, and the total amount of free disk space. The report also states the total amount of memory in the computer and the amount that is currently free (see Fig. 3-5).

## COMP

COMP, short for compare, is a useful utility for comparing the contents of two files to see if they differ. To use COMP, type

    COMP <*filename.ext*> <*filename.ext*>

44

```
C>chkdsk c:
Volume MAY001       created Mar 10, 1989 5:27a

 31107072 bytes total disk space
    53248 bytes in 3 hidden files
    69632 bytes in 29 directories
 18929664 bytes in 983 user files
   102400 bytes in bad sectors
 11952128 bytes available on disk

   655360 bytes total memory
   516960 bytes free

C>
```

**Fig. 3-5.** *The summary results from running CHKDSK on my C Drive.*

COMP can also be used with wildcard characters. See your DOS manual for more information.

## DEBUG

DEBUG is a very powerful DOS utility that should only be used by experienced PC users who know exactly what they are doing with it. DEBUG allows users to peek into memory and examine and modify information stored on disks. DEBUG can also be used to assemble and unassemble programs. If you feel you are an experienced PC user and are comfortable with Hex and addressing schemes, refer to your DOS manual for more information. If not, don't play with DEBUG.

## DISKCOMP

DISKCOMP is very similar to COMP, only instead of comparing files, it compares entire floppy disks. To use DISKCOMP, type

DISKCOMP <A:> <B:>

## FDISK

FDISK is a powerful utility that is used to partition hard drives. FDISK also can be used to view the current partition information for a hard drive. To do this, run FDISK and select option 4 - Display Partition Information. Be careful with this utility. If you select the wrong option, you can destroy information on the hard drive. See your DOS manual for more information.

## FORMAT

FORMAT is included here because it is often the best way to recover from an attack from a malicious program. Rather than trying to eliminate the bad program from your disk, you usually are better off to format over the disk and restore the information from backups. See your DOS manual for information on using FORMAT.

It is important to understand the difference between a high-level format and a low-level format when dealing with hard drives. There is only one formatting process necessary to format a floppy disk using FORMAT, but a hard disk must be low-level formatted and partitioned before it can be high-level formatted with FORMAT.

When reformatting a hard drive to purge it of a virus, it is recommended that you do a full format by starting with a low-level format. The FORMAT command only resets the boot sector, FAT(s), and root directory; a low-level format is needed to wipe all information off the disk. Alternately, you can use a wipe disk utility such as Norton's WipeDisk.

## SYS

SYS is a good utility to know because it can be useful in some problem situations. SYS copies the operating system files IBMDOS.COM and IBMBIO.COM or their MS-DOS equivalent from one drive to another. Note that SYS does not copy COMMAND.COM; you have to copy that file separately. To use SYS, type

```
SYS <C:>
```

The destination disk must be formatted for use as a system, or boot, disk in order for SYS to operate properly. See your DOS manual for more information.

## DOS AND MALICIOUS PROGRAMS

Throughout this chapter, various aspects of DOS have been explored, from the formatting of disk drives to utility programs. The reason for this, besides the fact that you can never know too much about your computer, is that by understanding the "playing field" and "rules" of your computer, you can anticipate and defend against attacks by malicious virus-type programs. This section pulls all of the information presented thus far into the subject of computer viruses, Trojan horses, and worms.

A key point to remember throughout all of this is that DOS limits you to detecting and eradicating malicious programs after they have been introduced to the computer and possibly done some damage. However, there are some preventative programs, that along with the safe computing practices discussed in Part I, can stop many common malicious programs dead in their tracks before they can do any damage. These preventative programs are covered in the next chapter.

In addition, there are many programs available that do many of the same things, and more, as the DOS utilities included in the previous section. These utility programs, such as Norton Utilities, Mace Utilities, and PC Tools are also covered in the next chapter. If you are really serious about keeping tabs on what is going on inside your computer or actually repairing damage, you will find these types of utilities indispensable.

However, now that you understand DOS, you will be able to identify the weak points that malicious programs are most likely to target for maximum damage. Many computer viruses attach to executable files, those with the .EXE and .COM extensions. This will cause an increase in the file's size as well as possibly altering the file creation/update date and time stamp (see Fig. 3-6). By using the COMP and/or DISKCOMP utilities, you can compare your working copies of programs with your original copies.

It is also possible, using ATTRIB, to make executable files read-only so that they cannot be written to. However, some programs modify themselves when you change setup information, so you will have to test the programs to see if they will run properly when set to read-only. It is a good idea to make your batch files, those with the .BAT extension, read-only. Some malicious programs alter batch files, such as AUTOEXEC.BAT.

CHKDSK is an excellent program to run everytime you use your computer. Pay particular attention to the number of hidden files and the amount of free memory. A regular system disk should have three hidden files: IBMBIO.COM, IBMDOS.COM, and the disk's volume label. Some copy-protected programs will create hidden files when installed on a hard drive. A new hidden file could indicate that a program is trying to hide itself or something else from you.

Users of AT class machines and higher, which have CMOS

```
    UTILS          <DIR>         3-10-89     5:45a
    NORTON         <DIR>         3-14-89     2:32a
    TYPESET        <DIR>         3-10-89     6:38a
    SYS            <DIR>         3-10-89     5:48a
    BAT            <DIR>         3-10-89     5:49a
    BKSHLF         <DIR>         3-10-89     5:49a
    XTPRO          <DIR>         3-10-89     5:49a
    WINDOWS        <DIR>         3-10-89     5:49a
    EE             <DIR>         3-10-89     5:51a
    PSPLUS         <DIR>         3-10-89     5:51a
    WORD4          <DIR>         3-10-89     5:51a
    UMI            <DIR>         3-10-89     5:52a
    PCPLUS         <DIR>         3-10-89     5:52a
    PBRUSH         <DIR>         3-10-89     7:27a
    PCKWIK         <DIR>         3-10-89     4:34p
    HG             <DIR>         3-14-89     4:40p
    COMMAND  COM    25307        3-17-87    12:00p
    COUNTRY  SYS    11285        3-17-87    12:00p
    CONFIG   SYS      179        4-01-89    10:36a
    AUTOEXEC BAT      469        4-01-89    10:36a
    SD       INI     2497        3-14-89     2:51a
    TREEINFO NCD      491        3-14-89     7:08p
           24 File(s)   11956224 bytes  free

C>
```

**Fig. 3-6.** *A directory showing COMMAND.COM. Note the size, date, and time entries.*

RAM, should make note of the current setup settings. There are a few computer viruses that can replicate into CMOS RAM, where they can survive indefinitely, even if you reboot and format all your drives. Should you suspect something funny is going on in your CMOS RAM, open your computer's case and disconnect the battery that is supplying the CMOS RAM with power for at least half an hour. When you reattach power and boot up, you will probably have to run your setup program again.

Many viruses target specific files that are common on most all IBM-PCs. An ideal example of this is COMMAND.COM. Of all the files on your PC to watch, COMMAND.COM is the most important. Should you notice any change in COMMAND.COM, delete it and get a new copy from your write-protected factory original DOS disk.

Some malicious programs erase files from your disk. When a file is erased, the information is not actually deleted from the disk.

Rather, the FAT is updated to show that the space taken up by the file is available for use. As long as you have not saved or copied any other files to the disk after the file is erased, it is possible to restore the file using an un-erase program, such as the UnErase program included with Norton Utilities.

Another very common host for a computer virus is the boot sector on a disk. Once the virus infects the boot sector, it can gain control of the computer as soon as it is turned on. Typically, the correct boot sector is placed elsewhere on the disk, usually in a hidden file. Until the virus is triggered, when the system is booted, the virus passes control to the actual boot sector and the computer boots normally. Once the virus is triggered, usually after having replicated itself a certain number of times, control is passed to the actual boot sector and then back to the virus, and it executes its instructions. The virus also might pass control to another malicious hidden program.

The easiest way to view the boot sector is with a disk utility software, such as Norton Utilities (see Fig. 3-7). You should probably check the boot sector, FAT, and root directory using a good utility program at least once a week. This way, you will be able to notice any changes, possibly before a virus triggers.

```
┌ Boot area ═══════════════════════════════════════════ Text format ═┐
│ Sector 0 in Boot Area                                  Offset 0, hex 0 │
│                                                                        │
│ ►δ4ÉIBM  3.3.....∩φ°<......·3 ╚Ä╜╝|..╖x6┼7.V.S╖+|╢│η¾&Ç=t.&è.¬è─Γ±..ëG.╟.+|√=│
│  .rgá.|ÿ≈&.|...|...|ú?|ú7|╖ ≈&.|ï.|.├H≈≤..7|╖.í?|Φf╖..Φ|r.ï/╢╝π)≤ªu◄ │
│ ►ì▓ ╝β}╢≤ªt.╝w}Φj2Σ=.^.Å.ÅD.=.╝ ╚}δδí..3π≈6|·╚ó<|í7|ú=|╖.í7|ΦIí.|*.;|@8.<|s│
│  .á<|PΦNXr╞(.<|t..7|≈&|.╪δ╨è..|è.²)ï.=|Ωp¼╚t".╖.=.δ≥3π≈6.|·τê.;|3π≈6<end-│
│  file-marker>|ê.*|ú9|╠.ï.9|▒.πμ6;|ï╨åθè.²)è6*|=.├◄ │
│ ►Non-System disk or disk error◄ │
│ ►Replace and strike any key when ready◄ │
│ ►◄ │
│ ►Disk Boot failure◄ │
│ ►IBMBIO  COMIBMDOS  COMÇU¬ │
│                                                                        │
│                                                                        │
│                                                                        │
│                                                                        │
│                                                                        │
│                                                                        │
│                                                                        │
│                        Press Enter to continue                         │
│1Help   2Hex    3Text   4Dir   5FAT   6Partn  7      8Choose 9Undo  10QuitNU│
```

**Fig. 3-7.** *A screen copy of the boot sector on my C drive obtained with Norton Utilities.*

Most viruses and Trojans aim much higher than corrupting individual files—they want to trash your entire disk or hard drive. The viruses simply use executable files as a host for replication. Once the virus is triggered, its main program is executed. The same is true for a Trojan, although it does not replicate.

The main program most likely will attempt to destroy the data on your disks in one of two ways; either by formatting the disk or by corrupting the FAT and/or boot sector. Fortunately, it is possible to recover from a formatted disk because a high-level format simply creates a new boot sector, zeroes out the FAT, and marks all files as erased. All data past the root directory is still intact, assuming no disk operations were performed following the format. None of the current malicious programs discussed in this book do a low-level hard drive format, which wipes the drive clean. The good disk utility programs, such as Norton Utilities, include an un-format option that can reconstruct the boot sector, FAT, and filenames. In the same manner, it is possible to recover from corrupted FATs.

However, in many cases, you do not want to restore the disk, even if it is possible. If the damage was caused by a virus, there are probably still active copies of it on the disk. However, if the damage was caused by a Trojan horse program that happened to reformat your drive while you were playing a new game, there is no reason why you should not try to restore the disk if you have the knowledge and tools. After all, if worse comes to worse, you can always reformat the disk and restore your data from backups.

Not all malicious programs attempt to damage information. It is possible for a virus or Trojan to cause hardware damage as well. For example, suppose a single-mode monitor is hooked up to a multi-mode graphics card and a malicious program causes the graphics card to shift into a higher resolution mode that the monitor does not support. It is conceivable that the monitor could overheat and suffer physical damage or even burst into flames.

Another possible target for physical damage is hard drives. A malicious program could repeatedly slam the hard drive's heads from the outermost cylinder to the innermost, causing greatly accelerated wear and tear on the drive. You might never know why your hard drive failed so quickly unless you discovered the malicious program; the search for which might possibly have been brought on by your keen observation that there had been an excessive amount of hard drive activity since you installed that new program.

## SUMMARY

By gaining a good understanding of the operating system that controls your IBM-PC, you can better understand how viruses and other malicious programs operate. After all, they are programs and must follow certain rules or they cannot run or do any damage. This chapter has covered the PC-DOS and MS-DOS environment from the perspective of understanding virus-type programs.

Using DOS' utilities such as CHKDSK, it is possible to monitor what is going on inside your PC. By keeping an eye out for any unusual changes in your system, you can prevent a malicious program from ever having the chance to trigger. If the program does trigger, you then have the option of restoring data from backups or attempting to recover lost files or reconstructing corrupted FATs and boot sectors.

If you are interested in learning more about DOS and your PC in general, the following books are recommended reading, both of which are listed in the bibliography.

Mace. *The Paul Mace Guide to Data Recovery*.

Norton. *Inside the IBM-PC*.

The next chapter discusses some programs and utilities that you can use in your defense against malicious virus-type programs.

# 4
# Anti-Viral Programs
# and Utilities

# Computer Viruses and the IBM-PC

THE THREAT OF COMPUTER VIRUSES, TROJAN HORSE programs, worms, and logic bombs has elicited a strong response in the form of anti-viral software. Most of these programs claim to protect your personal computer from damage should it be attacked by a malicious program. There are also several well known and well respected disk utility programs that can be used to help keep personal computers free of virus-type software.

This chapter covers currently available anti-viral programs and other related programs and hardware for the IBM-PC and compatibles. I have attempted to provide you with a comprehensive list of available products; however, computer virus software is a rapidly changing segment of the software market. By the time you read this, many of these programs will have been updated, some may no longer be available, and new ones may have been published. Also, please keep in mind that any pricing information given is subject to change.

In the following listings, the program or utility name, company or author, class of the software (commercial, shareware, etc.), and price are given followed by a brief description of the program. Many of the shareware programs are available for downloading from bulletin boards and information services such as CompuServe and Genie. Also, remember that several of the best shareware and public domain anti-viral programs and utilities are included in the disk accompanying this book.

## BOMBSQAD AND CHK4BOMB

Andy Hopkins
801 Wilson Road
Wilmington, DE 19803
Freeware - Somewhat limited distribution

Get these programs if you can. They are excellent programs designed to protect your PC from falling prey to Trojan horse programs. These programs are well respected and work. They have been out for several years; however, apparently their author has decided to restrict their future distribution. I was not able to obtain permission to include them in the disk that accompanies this book, otherwise they would be on it. You might be able to locate copies of these programs on bulletin boards, and they are currently included on the disk that accompanies Jerry FitzGerald's book *Online Auditing Using Microcomputers*, listed in the bibliography and in Appendix B.

BOMBSQAD, for Bomb Squad, is a RAM resident program that monitors all calls to the BIOS. The program displays the consequences of the call and asks if you want to allow the event to occur. CHK4BOMB, for Check for Bomb, scans a specified file and displays any text found in the files as well as warnings if the file contains any code that is capable of altering information stored on disks.

## C-4

InterPath
4423 Cheeney Street
Santa Clara, CA 95054
Commercial - $39.95

C-4 is a RAM resident program that monitors all activity on the PC for virus-like operations, such as writes to executable files or modifications to system files. If a C-4 suspects that a virus is active on the PC, C-4 will lock up the system and display a message giving the name of both the source file and the destination file involved in the viral replication.

## CHECKUP

Richard B. Levin
9405 Bustleton Avenue
Philadelphia, PA 19115
Shareware - $5 registration fee

Checkup is a good shareware anti-viral program. Checkup works on the principle that when a virus infects a PC, it causes a change in the code of the files it has infected. Checkup compares previously computed checksums for selected files with the same files currently on the disk. If Checkup identifies a checksum that does not match, then you know the file has been altered since the original checksum was computed. This way you can eliminate the infected file(s) before it has a chance to spread too far.

Checkup is available for downloading from Levin's bulletin board at (215) 333-6923.

## CORPORATE VACCINE (CERTUS)

FoundationWare
2135 Renrock
Cleveland, OH 44118
Commercial - $189

Corporate Vaccine, which is to be renamed CERTUS, is a quality commercial anti-viral product aimed at the corporate user (see Fig. 4-1). In addition to protecting the PC from viral infection, Vaccine also provides comprehensive logging and auditing tools. On boot up, Vaccine checks all programs to make sure they have not been altered. Before a program is allowed to run, Vaccine checks

**Fig. 4-1.** *Photo of FoundationWare's Corporate Vaccine.*

it once again. Vaccine prevents damaging writes to hard drives and can prevent writing or copying to floppy disks. Vaccine also creates a critical disk that contains copies of a hard drive's FAT, book sectors, partition information, and the computer's CMOS. Should the disk be reformatted or the CMOS battery die, the information can be restored using the critical disk. Vaccine also comes with a disk, known as the Blue Disk, that contains checksum information for a wide variety of popular shareware and public domain programs. You can compare the checksum of your copy of the program with that on the Blue Disk. And if they match, you can be relatively sure that you have a good, clean copy of the program.

## DATA PHYSICIAN

Digital Dispatch, Inc.
55 Lakeland Shores
St. Paul, MN 55043
Commercial - $199

Data Physician was one of the first high-end commercial anti-viral software packages developed and enjoys a good reputation. Data Physician consists of five separate programs. The package provides comprehensive protection. It will detect any unauthorized changes to files and intercept writes to the disk. Another one of the programs can be added to executable files so that they are self-checking each time they are run.

## DISK DEFENDER (HARDWARE)

Director Technologies
906 University Place
Evanston, IL 60201
Commercial - $240

The Disk Defender is a plug-in expansion card with an external control that is capable of hardware write-protecting all or part of a hard drive with a standard ST-506 or ST-412 interface (see Fig. 4-2). The control box is used to switch the write protection on and off, as well as displaying the status of the drive. Unchanging files and executable files can be stored in a write-protected partition of the drive while changing data can be stored elsewhere. The control

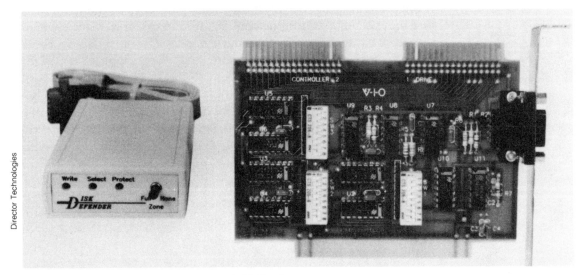

**Fig. 4-2.** *Director Technologies' Disk Defender.*

box can be removed so that the user cannot disable the write protection.

## DISK WATCHER

RG Software Systems
2300 Computer Avenue
Willow Grove, PA 19090
Commercial - $99.95

Disk Watcher is a RAM resident program that monitors all system activity and attempts to flag all activity indicative of a virus. When Disk Watcher thinks a virus is on the move, a message is displayed and the user has the option of stopping the event or allowing it to continue. The program also protects against more mundane events such as accidentally erasing a file.

## DR. PANDA UTILITIES

Panda Systems
801 Wilson Road
Wilmington, DE 19803
Commercial - $79.95

Dr. Panda is one of the best rated commercial anti-viral packages on the market and is capable of detecting viruses, Trojans, and worms. Dr. Panda includes six separate programs that can be mixed and matched to provide the desired level of security.

The first program, *Monitor*, is a memory resident program that traps all attempts to format a drive, write to the boot sector, or the initialization bytes of the FAT. Additional levels of security will prevent writes, reads, and verifications. The second program, *Physical*, checks a PC for any changes that might indicate the presence of a malicious program. The default files it checks include the system files and the boot sector. The user can customize the program to check other files, such as all EXE and COM files.

*Labtest* is used to scan any new program being installed for suspicious code. In addition, all text in the program is displayed. *Nobrain* is a utility written to check disks for the presence of the Pakistani-Brain virus. If found, the virus will be eliminated and the disk restored. The final program, *Tsrmon*, monitors all attempts by programs to load themselves into memory. If an unauthorized program tries to install itself as a RAM resident program, Tsrmon will flag it.

## FILE INTEGRITY CHECK

Gilmore Systems
P.O. Box 3831
Beverly Hills, CA 90212
Shareware - $15 registration fee

*Ficheck*, for File Integrity Check, is a good anti-viral program. Ficheck works by creating a reference disk that contains the date, time, size, attributes, and cyclic redundancy check of every file on your hard drive. When you run Ficheck again, it compares the reference disk to the same files on the hard drive. If there have been any changes, it lets you know. It is up to you to decide if the altered files are your doing or the result of a virus.

Chuck Gilmore, the author of Ficheck, also runs the *Virus Info Palladium* bulletin board at (213) 276-5263. You can download a copy of Ficheck from there, but you don't have to because Ficheck is one of the programs included on the disk accompanying this book. In addition, when you register your copy of Ficheck, you will receive a free copy of *Xficheck*, an extended version of Ficheck available only to registered users.

## FLU_SHOT +

Software Concepts Design
594 Third Avenue
New York, NY 10016
Shareware - $10 registration fee

Flu_Shot+ is one of the best known anti-viral programs around. Flu_Shot+ has a variety of features to protect your PC from being attacked by a virus or a Trojan. Using Flu_Shot +, you can read and write-protect individual files or classes of files. Flu_Shot+ also runs a checksum check on user selected files to see if they have been altered since the checksums were first computed. Flu_Shot+ will notify you if a program attempts to load itself into memory and become RAM resident.

Flu_Shot+ is truly one of the best programs for all-around protection. Ross Greenberg, the author of Flu_Shot +, runs a bulletin board at (212) 889-6438. Once again, you can download a copy of Flu_Shot+ from there, but you don't have to because it is included on the disk accompanying this book.

## GUARD CARD (HARDWARE)

NorthBank Corporation
10811 NorthBank Road
Richmond, VA 23333
Commercial - $194

The Guard Card is a plug-in expansion board that write-protects a hard drive. The card supports up to two drives, and works with any standard ST-506 hard drive controller.

## MACE UTILITIES

## MACE VACCINE

Paul Mace Software
499 Williamson Way
Ashland, OR 97520
Commercial:     $99 Mace Utilities
                $20 Mace Vaccine (if purchased separately)

Mace Utilities is a comprehensive disk utility program that is similar in many respects to Norton Utilities. Mace Vaccine is included with Mace Utilities or can be purchased separately. Mace Vaccine write-protects critical areas of a disk and will prompt you before allowing any writes to its protected area. Mace Vaccine can also be configured to write-protect the disk from all direct writes that bypass DOS. I've heard many good things about Mace Utilities, and though I'm a Norton user myself, I encourage you to check it out before buying a disk utility program. Paul Mace is also the author of the excellent book *The Paul Mace Guide to Data Recovery*.

## NORTON UTILITIES ADVANCED EDITION
## NORTON UTILITIES STANDARD EDITION

Peter Norton Computing, Inc.
100 Wilshire Boulevard
9th Floor
Santa Monica, CA 90401
Commercial:     $150 Advanced Edition
                $100 Standard Edition

Norton Utilities is a legendary disk utility that, while not containing any anti-viral programs, is very useful for protecting and repairing your disk from damage caused not only by viruses and Trojans, but by human error as well. The Advanced Edition includes *Norton Disk Doctor*, an excellent program that can find and correct almost any logical or physical errors on floppy disks and hard drives. Another program allows you to view the boot sector, FAT, and root directory including all hidden files. In short, Norton Utilities is an excellent program. I highly recommend it; its UnErase feature has recovered many accidentally erased files for me over the years.

## VACCINE

World Wide Data Corporation
17 Battery Place
New York, NY 10004
Commercial - $79.95

Vaccine comes with two supporting programs, Antidote and Checkup. Vaccine is a RAM resident program. It monitors system activity and notifies you if any program tries to modify the disk in a suspicious manner. *Antidote* scans the disk for the presence of viruses that have been identified by World Wide Data. *Checkup* maintains a record of executable files and informs you if any of them have been altered.

5

# Virus-Proofing
# Your PC

T HE PAST TWO CHAPTERS HAVE EXPLORED THE MANY options that a user of an IBM-PC can employ to protect his system from infection by a computer virus. However, with all the available options, it can be difficult to determine exactly what steps should be taken and how often. In this chapter, the information presented in earlier chapters is used to develop a rational methodology for the average IBM-PC user who is concerned about the possibility of being infected or attacked by a malicious program, but at the same time, does not want to give up the benefits of an open user community.

## BACKUP

Before going any further with the discussion of viruses and related programs, it is very important that I stress the necessity of maintaining thorough usable backups of all important programs, data, and other files. I'm sure that you have heard many times before now that backup is essential; now it is even more so. Viruses, Trojans, worms, and logic bombs have now joined with hard drive crashes, worn out media, fire, and flood as reasons to maintain backups. The goal of backups, when dealing with virus-type programs, is to be able to restore clean, uninfected copies of programs, batch files, and data (see Fig. 5-1).

While it is often possible to reconstruct a hard drive that has been corrupted by a virus or Trojan, in many cases it is not the wise thing to do. There is a good possibility that there are other copies

|  |  |
|---|---|
| ☐ Week 1 | Clean backup |
| ☐ Week 2 | Clean backup |
| ☐ Week 3 | Clean backup |

**Virus Infects System**

|  |  |
|---|---|
| ☐ Week 4 | Infected backup |
| ☐ Week 5 | Infected backup |

**Virus Triggers**

**Restore From Week 3 Backup**

*Fig. 5-1. Routine backups are very important, especially when your system gets infected by a virus-type program.*

of the virus on the disk or that data has been altered that you might not notice. Therefore, once attacked by a malicious program, you should attempt to restore data. However, if there are a few valuable files on the affected disk that you do not have backed up, you can attempt to recover them.

It is also important to keep several copies of backups, staggered in time, so that you can restore files from one week ago, two weeks ago, one month ago, or even three to six months ago. The reason for this is that a virus or logic bomb might have been in your system for quite a while before it was triggered, and you want to be able to restore from a point in time before your system was infected. Because of the inherent costs of maintaining so many backups, both in terms of time and money, it is important that you develop a backup method that works and that you will follow. This section explores several methods of backup, both for floppy disks and hard drives.

## Floppy Disk Based Computers

If you are running your computer without a hard drive, you only have to maintain adequate copies of disks that change, such as your data disks. The first thing you should do is isolate your programs from your data. Keep all your executable files on write-protected floppy disks, and maintain backup copies of your data disks. For example, do not store text files on your word processor's program disk. Also, make sure you are using write-protected copies of your factory master disks for everyday work, not the factory masters themselves.

Once you have configured all of the program disks, make backup copies of them. Now all you have to do is allocate approximately five floppy disks to each data disk for backup. Make one copy now. In one week, assuming you have used the data disk, make another copy of the data disk on another backup disk, and so on. In five weeks, you should have weekly copies of each of your data disks. Now start rotating the backup disks.

Adjust the number of backups and the time between backups to suit your needs. Backups going back one month at one week intervals should be the minimum you consider. Some people make daily backups of their data disks going back a few months.

## Hard Drives

Hard drives are convenient in many ways, but they can pose problems when trying to backup the massive amounts of information they can store. Some people try to get around backing up the entire contents of their hard drives by only backing up files that have changed since their last backup or by only backing up data since they already have floppy disk copies of all their programs. This is fine as long as you have a complete one-time backup of your hard drive that is recent within at least three months.

There are several methods of backing up hard drives. The pros and cons of each method are discussed in the following paragraphs.

**Floppy**    The least expensive method of backing up a hard drive is by copying the files to floppy disks. All of the equipment needed is built right into the computer. DOS even includes a simple backup and restoration program set that enables you to backup files that are larger than a single floppy disk over multiple floppy disks. There are also several programs available, such as Fifth Generation's *FastBack*, that will back up your hard drive onto floppy disks much faster than the DOS backup utility.

Regardless of whether you use DOS' BACKUP and RE-STORE commands or purchase a commercial floppy disk backup program, backing up onto floppy disks is by far the least expensive means to backup your hard drive. If you have high density drives, by all means use them; the less disks you have to swap, the less tedious backing up becomes.

**Tape**    There are several tape backup systems on the market, ranging in price from $200 to $1500, and the tape cartridges cost between $20 and $50. But, tape backup is one of the most effortless methods available to backup a hard drive. Using a tape backup is easy, just insert the tape cartridge into the drive, run a backup program, and wait.

Tape drive can be mounted internally or housed externally. Some require a separate controller board while others will attach to your existing floppy controller. Tape backup should be one of your primary choices if you have a large capacity hard drive and are planning on making frequent backups.

**Alternative Methods**    While floppy and tape are the most common methods of backing up a hard drive, they are by no means the only method. Some people install a second hard drive in their computer for use only as a backup. From a security standpoint, that is not a very good idea. If anything happens to the computer, the backup goes with it. Also, a virus could very easily replicate itself onto the backup hard drive.

Write-Once, Read-Many optical disks are rapidly becoming a popular method to backup a hard drive. With storage capacities of over 150 megabytes, it is possible to store two or three full backups of an average hard drive on one optical disk.

Backing up your hard drive is a lot like insurance, you hate to pay the premiums but are sure glad you did when disaster strikes. Regardless of the method you choose to backup your hard drive, make sure you follow through by keeping timely, organized backups of all your important files. That way, when and if you are the target of a malicious program, or a more mundane calamity such as a user error, you will be able to quickly restore your computer system to operating condition.

## PREVENTATIVE COMPUTING

This section describes many methods that you can use to prevent disaster from striking in the form of a malicious virus-type program unleashed in your PC. The key word in this discussion is *preventative*. Preventative computing involves several steps that involve concepts discussed in earlier chapters, such as having a good understanding or your PC and its operating system, keeping adequate backups, using good judgment when acquiring programs for use on your PC, thoroughly testing new programs, and being aware of any sudden changes in the operation of your PC.

Unless you are putting your personal computer system together from scratch, you probably have a great deal of software from a variety of sources. Any software that you have been using regularly for over six months without any complications is probably clean. However, keep in mind that there are a wide variety of viruses and Trojans that might not trigger for a year or more, so do not rule out the possibility of an older program being the source of infection.

There are two main ways of obtaining new software: 1) on disk or 2) via telecommunications. Disk based software is predominantly commercial although shareware, public domain, and other types of software are also often distributed on disk. With regard to personal computers, telecommunications usually refers to telephone line modem communications. Programs are downloaded from a remote computer to your PC and are usually shareware, freeware, and public domain.

When you get a new program that is distributed on disk, the first thing you should do is make sure it is write-protected. When the disk is write-protected, the disk drive mechanism will write to or alter information stored on the disk. To write-protect a 5¼-inch disk, cover the write-protect notch with a write-protect tab. With 3½-inch disks, open the sliding tab so that you can see through the tiny square opening.

You should write-protect all of your master copies of programs. Only use backup copies of the master disks when running the programs or for installing the programs on your hard drive. For maximum security when making backup copies of your write-protected master disks, turn off your PC for at least thirty seconds. Then boot the computer from a clean write-protected DOS disk (obviously, if you are making a backup copy of your master DOS disk(s), use the write-protected original). Then use DISKCOPY to make a copy of the master disks. You can also use DISKCOMP to compare the backup copy with the master disk.

You can now run a Trojan horse detector program such as CHK4BOMB, LABTEST (part of Dr. Panda Utilities), and CHKANSI on the files on the disk. These programs will let you know if any of the files on the disk contain code that is capable of harming data stored in your PC. These Trojan detector programs have to be used with some common sense.

Every program that they flag does not contain a Trojan or a virus. These programs simply let you know if the program is capable of altering data, not that the program is malicious. If you run CHK4BOMB on a copy of Norton Utilities, warnings will pop up all over because Norton Utilities is capable of altering information. However, if you run one of these programs on a "normal" applications program, such as a spell checker for your word processor, and discover that the program contains the code necessary to reformat your hard drive along with a message such as "Ha Ha! Your hard drive's history," you should be very wary about this program. I for one would never use it, destroy all copies of it, and notify the source that I obtained it from.

Be very suspicious of illegal copies of commercial software and programs that come with no documentation or information about the author. Also, if a program's file size is inconsistent with its function, be wary. For example, if a full-featured word processing program takes up only 10K of disk space, something is probably wrong. The bottom line is to be careful and use common sense. However, do not let the threat of computer viruses scare you from trying new programs.

## PLAYING IT SAFE

There are a great many ways to protect your computer system from infection by a computer virus or worm and/or attack by a Trojan or logic bomb. The most extreme method is to write all your own software from scratch and never use any other programs on your PC. However, this is an extreme solution for most of us. Therefore, this section discusses ways to practice "safe computing" while still enjoying the benefits of an open information exchange in the PC community.

The previous section emphasized screening programs for code that could be malicious. However, if you don't have a screening program or you decide that a program might have a valid reason to alter information, you might want to go ahead and run the program on you PC. The key objective at this point is to run the program in an environment where it will do the least damage and to keep track of the other files stored on your disks for possible modifications.

The safest way to run a new program is on a floppy disk. That way, if the program does contain a simple malicious virus or Trojan, it might be contained to the floppy disk. If the program is too large to be run on a single floppy disk, you can run it on your hard drive, but put the program and its associated files in their own sub-directory. Some viruses and Trojans are not capable of harming information located in other directories.

After running the program, check several key files to see if they have been altered. These files include COMMAND.COM, IBMBIO. COM, IBMDOS.COM, AUTOEXEC.BAT, and any other files you wish to use. The operating system files should never be altered unless you know exactly what you are doing, and no program should alter them without informing you first. Should you find them altered, assume the worst, wipe the disk clean, and restore your files from a backup. Alterations to other non-operating system files will have to be judged on a case by case basis. If at any point you believe that a program is doing something that it shouldn't, stop right then and contact the company or author to find out if the program is behaving normally.

There are several commercial and shareware programs available that can help you detect when a program is attempting to do something dangerous, such as formatting a disk. Flu__Shot + is one of the best of this class of anti-viral programs and is included on the disk accompanying this book. See the disk's manual for more information on Flu__Shot + .

Another approach used by anti-viral programs is to check to see if any files have been altered since the last time the program was run. File Integrity Checker, FICHECK, is an excellent example of this type of program. FICHECK will let you know if any of the files on your hard drive have been altered since FICHECK was last used. This is an excellent way to detect infection by a computer virus. FICHECK uses a sophisticated checksumming method to determine if any files have been altered. FICHECK is also included on the disk accompanying this book; see the manual for more information.

Another very useful tool to have is a disk utility program such as Norton Utilities or Mace Utilities. Both are excellent programs and come with thorough documentation. I personally use Norton Utilities Advanced Edition and am very happy with it. With a disk utility package, you can examine the boot sector, FAT, and directory entries, making virus detection much easier. In addition, Norton's Format Remove and Mace's UnFormat can be used to recover information from a hard drive that has been reformatted. They also include programs to recover erase files and other handy utilities.

If you are interested in using a disk utility program and learning more about disks and DOS, I recommend the following books, which are included in the bibliography:

*The Paul Mace Guide To Data Recovery* by Paul Mace.

*Inside the IBM PC* by Peter Norton.

*PC Magazine DOS Power Tools* by Paul Somerson.

The best way to combat viruses and virus related programs is by becoming familiar with your PC. These books will provide you with a solid foundation.

The next several paragraphs present some general guidelines that sum up most of the information presented over the past several chapters. By following these guidelines, you should be able to keep your exposure to computer viruses and related programs to an acceptable minimum.

If you have a drive, format it as a system disk and boot from the hard drive, not from a floppy unless you are sure it is clean. The best way to create a clean floppy boot disk is to use write-protected factory master copies of the operating system and duplicate it using DISKCOPY. If you want to add files to the boot disk, such as an AUTOEXEC.BAT, create them manually using

EDLIN, the line editor provided with DOS or simply type the BAT file in directly from the keyboard using the COPY command. For example:

1. Type COPY CON: A:AUTOEXEC.BAT and press Return.
2. Type the contents of the file. Press Return at the end of each line.
3. Press F6 when done.

The file will now exist on the floppy disk in Drive A and will contain what you typed in after the COPY command and before you pressed the F6 key. When you install the operating system on your hard drive, make sure you use the write-protected factory master copies. The same rationales in the previous paragraph apply here. (Refer to Chapter 2 for additional information about "Preventive Computing.")

## SUMMARY

The IBM PC is an enormously popular standard personal computer system. Because of this, we enjoy a wide range of programs available for our machines; however, we are also the targets of malicious programs such as viruses, Trojans, worms, and logic bombs. However, by using the knowledge gained in this chapter and the rest of this book, you can fight back against these malicious programs. Fortunately, the likelihood of your being attacked by a malicious program is very low provided you take some care in what programs you run on your PC.

With this book and its accompanying Anti-Viral disk, you should be able to maintain an adequate defense against malicious programs. I hope that one day this book is not needed by anyone except as a curiosity from a bygone era of personal computing, but I sadly think that will not be the case for the foreseeable future. The one good thing about computer viruses is that they are forcing users of personal computers to learn more about the inner workings of their machines. For it is only through a more educated user community that the scourge of malicious programs will ever be eradicated.

# A
# Useful DOS Utilities

This appendix lists numerous DOS utilities that are useful in combating malicious, virus-type programs. Refer to your DOS manual or a good book on DOS for specific information on using these programs.

**ATTRIB**   ATTRIB is used to set or reset the read-only attribute; it can also be used to display the current setting.

**BACKUP and RESTORE**   To help with the task of backing up files from your hard drive, DOS includes a rudimentary backup and restoration system. BACKUP is used to copy the files to a floppy disk and RESTORE is used to get them back.

**CHKDSK**   CHKDSK is one of the most valuable DOS utilities. CHKDSK analyzes the FAT, directories, and files on a disk and produces a disk and memory status report. CHKDSK can also be used to fix simple errors in the directory or FAT.

**COMP**   COMP, short for compare, is a useful utility for comparing the contents of two files to see if they differ.

**DEBUG**   DEBUG is a powerful utility that allows users to look into memory to examine or modify information stored on disk. DEBUG can also be used to assemble and unassemble programs.

**DISKCOMP**   DISKCOMP is very similar to COMP, only instead of comparing files, it compares entire floppy disks.

**FDISK**   FDISK is a powerful utility that is used to partition hard drives and can be used to view the current partition information for a hard drive. To do this, run FDISK and select option 4 - Display Partition Information. Be careful with this utility. If you select the wrong option, you can destroy information on the hard drive.

**FORMAT**   FORMAT is included here because it is often the best way to recover from an attack from a malicious program. Rather than trying to eliminate the bad program from your disk, you usually are better off to format over the disk and restore the information from backups. When dealing with a hard drive, it is better to do a low-level format first, partition the drive, and then do a high-level format.

**SYS**   SYS copies the operating system files IBMDOS.COM and IBM-BIO.COM, or their MS-DOS equivalent, from one drive to another. Note that SYS does not copy COMMAND.COM; you have to copy that file separately.

# B

# Sources

This appendix contains the addresses of most of the companies and organizations mentioned in the book, listed in alphabetical order.

**Digital Dispatch**
55 Lakeland Shores
St. Paul, MN 55043
(612) 436-1000

**Director Technologies**
906 University Place
Evanston, IL 60201
(312) 491-2334

**FoundationWare**
2135 Renrock
Cleveland, OH 44118
(800) 722-8737

**Gilmore Systems**
P.O. Box 3831
Beverly Hills, CA 90212-0831
(213) 275-8006

**InterPath**
4423 Cheeney Street
Santa Clara, CA 95054
(404) 988-3832

**Jerry FitzGerald &**
**Associates**
506 Barkentine Lane
Redwood City, CA 94065
(415) 591-5676

**NorthBank Corporation**
10811 NorthBank Road
Richmond, VA 23333
(804) 741-7591

**Panda Systems**
> 801 Wilson Road
> Wilmington, DE 19803
>
> (302) 764-4722

**Paul Mace Software**
> 499 Williamson Way
> Ashland, OR 97520
> (503) 488-0224

**Peter Norton Computing**
> 100 Wilshire Boulevard
> 9th Floor
> Santa Monica, CA 90401
> (213) 319-2000

**RG Software Systems**
> 2300 Computer Avenue
> Willow Grove, PA 19090
> (215) 659-5300

**Software Concepts Design**
> 594 Third Avenue
> New York, NY 10016
> (503) 488-0224

**World Wide Data Corporation**
> 17 Battery Place
> New York, NY 10004
> (212) 422-4100

# Glossary

This glossary is a comprehensive list designed to provide you with brief definitions of computer virus-related terms. Check the index to see if the term you are looking up is referenced in the main text of the book.

**analog**   A signal that varies in a continuous manner (e.g. voice, music, and voltage and currents that vary in a continuous manner). See digital.

**ANSI**   Acronym for *American National Standards Institute*. The principal standards development organization in the United States.

**argument**   A variable expression that follows a command.

**ASCII**   Acronym for *American Standard Code for Information Interchange*. Also USASCII. A seven bit code established by ANSI to achieve compatibility between digital devices.

**assembly language**   A low-level, high-speed computer language consisting of mnemonics and operands which are converted, or assembled, to machine code. See machine code, BASIC, C.

**asynchronous**   Also called Start-Stop transmission. Digital signals which are being sent as groups of a specified length with start and stop bit indicators at the beginning and end of each group.

Usually used when time intervals between transmitted groups might be uneven. See synchronous.

**BASIC**   Acronym for *Beginner's All-purpose Symbolic Instruction Code*. A high-level computer language included with most personal computers. See C, assembly language, machine code.

**baud**   A unit of signaling speed equal to the number of discrete signal events per second. Baud is equal to BPS only if each signal event represents exactly one bit. See BPS, bit.

**BBS**   Also called CBBS, PBBS, Mailbox. Abbreviation for *Bulletin Board System*. An automated computer system which can be controlled from a remote location, usually with another computer system, over the phone lines using a modem. Usually capable of sending and receiving messages and files. See modem.

**boot sector**   A sector on a bootable floppy or hard disk that contains a small program that starts the process of loading the operating system.

**binary**   A number system based on the powers of 2. The only characters are a "0" and a "1". Binary digits are easily transmitted and stored in electronic equipment. See bit, hex, octal.

**bit**   Abbreviation for *BInary digiT*; either a "0" or a "1".

**buffer**   Memory space set aside for temporary storage of data until recalled, processed, or permanently stored.

**byte**   A grouping of eight bits. See nybble, octet.

**C**   A high-speed, high-level computer language. See BASIC, machine code, assembly language.

**control character**   A special character recognized by the computer as having a special meaning. Usually sent by pressing a control key and the appropriate character on the keyboard simultaneously.

**CMOS**   Abbreviation for *Complementary Metal Oxide Semiconductor*. A low-power semiconductor that is used for RAM in AT class IBM-PCs for permanent storage of setup and configuration information.

**CPU**   Abbreviation for Central Processing Unit. The "brains" of a computer. Responsible for directing the flow of data throughout the computer and performing calculations.

**data**   The digital information that is being transmitted or received.

**demodulation**   The process of receiving data from a modulated signal. See modulation, modem.

**digital**   A discrete or discontinuous signal whose various states are identified with specified values. See analog.

**DOS**   Acronym for *Disk Operating System*.

**EBCDIC**   Acronym for *Extended Binary Coded Decimal Interchange Code*. An eight-level character code developed for IBM and used primarily in their mini and mainframe computer systems. See ASCII.

**FAT**   Acronym for *File Allocation Table*. Used by DOS to keep track of the location of files on disks.

**freeware**   A program distributed without charge, but still under the control of the author.

**full duplex**   Simultaneous two-way independent transmission in both directions on separate channels. See simplex, half duplex.

**half duplex**   A communications circuit designed for transmission in either direction on two separate channels but not both directions simultaneously. See full duplex, simplex.

**hard drive**   Also called fixed disk or Winchester drive. A rigid disk magnetic storage device permanently sealed in a hermetic container which can store large amounts of data; usually (for personal computers) 20 to 150 megabtyes.

**hardware**   Physical equipment as opposed to programs and data.

**hex**   Abbreviation for hexadecimal. A number system based on the powers of 16. Characters are 0-9 and A-F. See binary, octal.

**IC**   Acronym for Integrated Circuit.

**I/O**   Acronym for Input/Output. Used in reference to any system or function that deals with sending and receiving data.

**logic bomb**   A program or an addition to an existing program that executes when triggered by a specific event, such as a certain date.

**machine code**   A low-level, high-speed computer language consisting of the actual binary instructions acted upon by the computer. See assembly language, BASIC, C.

**modem**   Contraction for *MOdulator/DEModulator*. A device that modulates transmitted signals and demodulates received signals. Serves as an interface between an analog communications system (such as the telephone) and digital devices (such as computers). See modulation, demodulation.

**modulation**   The process of adding a signal to a carrier to transmit information. Can be used in voice communications, but refers to digital data in the context of personal computer communications.

**nybble**   A group of four bits. One half of a byte. Represented by a single hex character. See hex.

**octal**   A number system based on the powers of 8. Characters are 0-7. See hex, binary.

**octet**   A group of eight bits. See byte, nybble.

**peripheral**   Any device which can be connected to a computer system to expand its operating capabilities.

**protocol**   A formal set of rules which dictate the format, timing, and other parameters of message exchange between two or more devices.

**RAM**   Acronym for *Random Access Memory*. Electronic memory that may be read from and written to. However, once power is removed, all data is lost.

**ROM**   Acronym for *Read Only Memory*. Electronic memory that may be read from but not written to. Data is permanently retained. Most ROMs can be erased with UV light, so the top window of the ROM chip is covered with a label or sticker to block all light.

**shareware**   A program that can be legally distributed and used contingent on registering the program with the author for a fee if the program is useful.

**simplex**   Operation over a single channel in one direction at a time. See full duplex, half duplex.

**software**   The program and procedures that control the operation of hardware systems.

**synchronous**   Transmission which the data is transmitted at a fixed rate with the transmitter and receiver synchronized. This eliminates the need for start and stop elements used with asynchronous transmission. See asynchronous.

**Trojan horse**   A program hidden within a host program that is triggered when the host program is executed.

**virus**   A program that attaches to other programs or files and replicates, copying itself to other files, disks, or computer systems.

**worm**   A malicious program that moves through memory, changing data in its path.

# Bibliography

This section of the book contains a sizeable listing of books and articles dealing with the subject of computer viruses in some way. This is not a comprehensive listing of all the published material on computer viruses. A comprehensive listing would make it very difficult for you to select the works that are of most interest to you, because you would have to spend a lot of time locating and examining them. Rather, the material selected here reinforces and expands upon the concepts presented in this book, as well as presents information that was helpful in the process of preparing this book.

If you are interested in keeping abreast of the latest news about computer viruses, keep an eye out for articles on the subject in major newspapers and computer magazines. Several computer virus related articles have appeared in *The Wall Street Journal*, *The New York Times*, and *The Washington Post*, as well as in local newspapers. For more technical information geared towards the personal computer user, *Byte*, *PC Magazine*, *PC Week*, and *PC World* are reliable sources.

## BOOKS

Berliner, Don. *Managing Your Hard Disk*. Indianapolis: QUE, 1986.
Burger, Ralf. *Computer Viruses: A High-Tech Disease*. Grand Rapids: Abacus, 1988.
DeVoney, Chris. *Using PC-DOS*. Indianapolis: QUE, 1986.
Fites, Philip et al. *The Computer Virus Crisis*. New York: Van Nostrand Reinhold, 1989.

FitzGerald, Jerry. *Online Auditing Using Microcomputers*. Redwood City: Jerry FitzGerald & Associates, 1987.

IBM. *DOS Reference Manual*. Boca Raton: IBM, 1988.

_____. *DOS Technical Reference Manual*. Boca Raton: IBM, 1988.

Mace, Paul. *The Paul Mace Guide to Data Recovery*. New York: Brady, 1988.

Norton, Peter. *Inside the IBM-PC*. New York: Brady, 1986.

Roberts, Ralph. *Computer Viruses*. Greensboro: Compute! Books, 1988.

Somerson, Paul. *PC Magazine DOS Power Tools: Techniques, Tricks, and Utilities*. New York: Bantam, 1988.

## ARTICLES

Alexander, Michael. "Worm Dissection Leads Some to Say Attack was Deliberate." *Computerworld*. 05 December 1988: 01.

_____. "Friday the 13th Virus Back in Silicon Valley." *Computerworld*. 23 January 1989: 04.

Bunzel, Rick. "Flu Season." *Connect*. Summer 1988: 40.

Butterfield, Jim. "The Amiga Virus." *Compute!*. March 1988: 48

Dembart, Lee. "Attack of the Computer Virus." *Discover*. November 1984: 90.

Elmer-DeWitt, Philip. "Invasion of the Data Snatchers." *Time*. 26 September 1988: 62.

Greenberg, Ross. "The Aftermath of a Worm Attack." *UNIX Today!*. 14 November 1988: 01.

Greenstein, Irwin and Neubarth, Michael. "Virus Plagues DOD Network." *Management Information Systems Week*. 07 November 1988: 52.

Gross, Steve. "Computer Virus." *Omni*. June 1986: 35.

Hafner, Katherine M. et al. "Is Your Computer Secure?" *Business Week*. 01 August 1988: 64.

Honan, Patrick. "Beware: It's Virus Season." *Personal Computing*. July 1988: 36.

Howard, Ron. "The Real Threats Posed by So-Called Computer Viruses." *Digital News*. 09 January 1989: 36.

Gantz, John. "Of Unix, Worms, and Viruses: Science Fiction Becomes Real." *Infoworld*. 21 November 1988: 40.

Gianatasio, David. "Campers Caught (Red-Handed?) In Virus Prank." *Digital Review*. 09 January 1989: 03.

Jackson, Kelly. "Virus Alters Networking." *Communications Week*. 14 November 1988: 01.

_____. "Virus Fosters Growth In Sales Of Security Products." *Communications Week*. 21 November 1988: 16.

Jenkins, Avery. "System Managers Battle Vermin." *Digital Review*. 19 December 1988: 57.

Joyce, Edward J. "Time Bomb: Inside the Texas Virus Trail." *Computer Decisions*. December 1988: 38.

Kask, Alex. "Computer Viruses Are as Easy To Prevent as the Common Cold." *Infoworld*. 12 December 1988: 49.

Marbach, William D. et al. "Is Your Computer Infected?" *Newsweek*. 01 February 1988: 48.

Marshall, Eliot. "The Scourge of Computer Viruses." *Science*. 08 April 1988: 133.

Marshall, Martin. "Virus Control Center is Proposed." *Infoworld*. 12 December 1988: 08.

McAfee, John D. "Managing the Virus Threat." *Computerworld*. 13 February 1989: 89.

_____. "The Virus Cure." *Datamation*. 15 February 1989: 29.

Menkus, Belden. "The Computer Virus Danger Grows." *Modern Office Technology*. February 1989: 38.

Parker, Rachel. "Beware of Companies That Fan Flames of Computer Virus Fear." *Infoworld*. 23 January 1989: 40.

Pournelle, Jerry. "Dr. Pournelle vs. The Virus." *Byte*. July 1988: 197.

Puttre, Michael. "For MIS, The Virus Lingers." *InformationWEEK*. 14 November 1988: 25.

Roeckl, Chris. "User Organization Offers Virus Prescription." *Communications Week*. 16 January 1989: 24.

Rosenhouse, Helene. "Vaccine Inoculates Against System Ills." *InformationWEEK*. 24 October 1988: 19.

Rubenking, Neil J. "Infection Protection." *PC Magazine*. 25 April 1989: 193.

Schneiker, Henry. "Protecting A System From Bugs." *Digital News*. 23 January 1989: 23.

Stefanac, Suzanne. "Mad Macs." *MacWorld*. November 1988: 92.

Synergy, Michael. "Cyber Terrorists Viral Hitmen." *Reality Hackers*. Winter 1988: 68.

Wallace, Louis R. "Vanquishing the Viruses." *Amiga World*. November 1988: 48.

Wellman, David A. "Thou Shalt Not Violate Network Security." *InformationWEEK*. 12 December 1988: 44.

Wilder, Clinton. "Cashing In on Virus Anxieties." *Computerworld*. 21 November 1988: 01.

# PART III

# Anti-Viral
# Utility Disk

Part III explains how to use the IBM-PC Anti-Viral Utility disk located at the back of this book. Detailed instructions are provided and the documentation file that accompany each utility are reprinted here for convenience and easy access by the user.

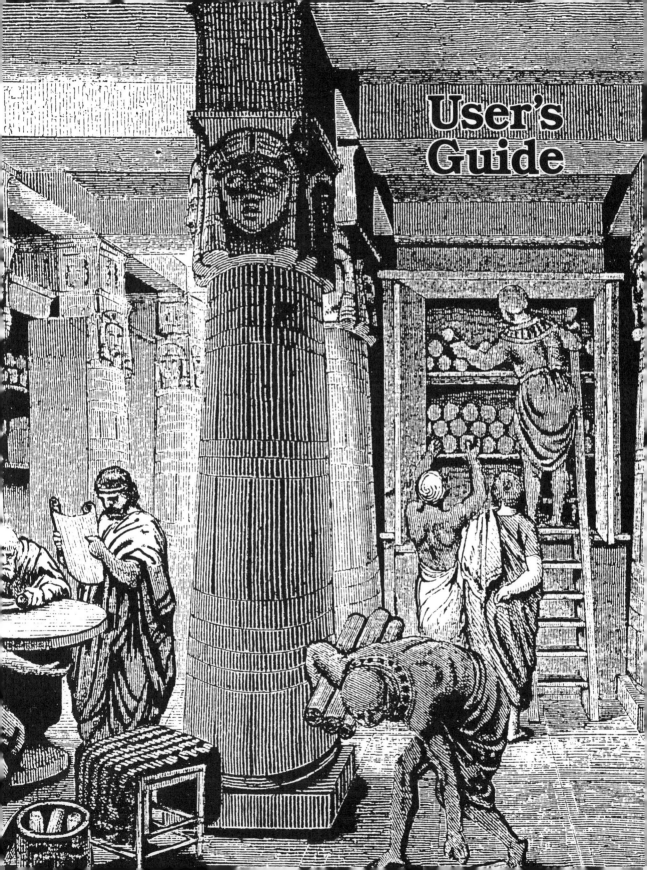

User's Guide

## Anti-Viral Utility Disk

**E**NCLOSED IN THE BACK OF THIS BOOK IS A DISKETTE containing numerous public domain and shareware anti-viral programs for the IBM-PC and compatibles. With these programs, you will be able to insulate your PC from the effects of computer viruses, Trojan horses, worms, and logic bombs.

I would like to thank Ross Greenberg, author of Flu__Shot +; Chuck Gilmore, author of File Integrity Checker, Check ANSI, and CAWARE; and Jerry FitzGerald, author of the book *Online Auditing Using Microcomputers*, for allowing me to include their programs on this diskette and/or supplying me with files to include on this diskette.

Many of the programs on the enclosed diskette are shareware. Their authors have graciously permitted their programs to be distributed on this diskette for your benefit. Should you find any of the shareware programs to be of use, you are encouraged to register with the author of the program. Instructions on how to register are included in the documentation files for the programs. It is also possible that new versions of some programs might be released by the time you get this book, so if you like a particular program, you should contact the author for the latest version.

The disk is formatted as a standard 360K data disk using PC-DOS 3.3, and should be readable by all IBM-PCs or compatibles with a 5¼-inch disk drive. This disk is readable on both 360K and 1.2 Mb floppy drives. If you have only 3½-inch drives, you will have to copy the files on this disk to a 3½-inch disk so that your computer can read them.

The first thing you should do is make a backup copy of the enclosed disk. To make a backup copy of the disk, use the DOS utility DISKCOPY. First, put your DOS disk in Drive A or change to your DOS directory on your hard drive. At the DOS prompt, type:

```
DISKCOPY A: A:
```

then press Return. Following the directions on the screen, put the enclosed disk into Drive A and press Return. When prompted, remove the enclosed disk, put a blank disk into Drive A, and press Return. When asked if you desire additional copies, answer No unless you do want to make another copy of the disk, in which case you will have to go through this procedure again. You should put the enclosed master copy in a safe place and use the copy you just made from now on.

If you want to be certain that you have an identical copy of the enclosed disk, you can use DISKCOMP to compare it with the copy you made. DISKCOMP is a DOS utility; to use it, type:

DISKCOMP A: A:

then press Return. When prompted, insert the enclosed master disk into Drive A and press Return. Do the same with the copied disk. If you get any errors, try copying the enclosed disk again onto a different disk.

## DISK ORGANIZATION

The disk contains twelve files, four of which are stored in a compressed, archive format. Figure M-1 shows the results of a CHKDSK performed on the enclosed disk with the /V option. You can run CHKDSK on your copy by typing:

CHKDSK A: /V

then press Return. Make sure your copied disk is in Drive A.

```
Volume IBM_VIRUS   created Mar 27, 1989 12:00a
Directory A:\
      A:\IBM_VIRU.S
Directory A:\CAWARE
      A:\CAWARE\CAWARE.EXE
Directory A:\CHKANSI2
      A:\CHKANSI2\CHKANSI.EXE
Directory A:\FICHECK5
      A:\FICHECK5\FICHECK5.EXE
Directory A:\FSP_152
      A:\FSP_152\FSP_152.EXE
Directory A:\MISC_PRG
      A:\MISC_PRG\CBIN.DOC
      A:\MISC_PRG\CBIN.EXE
      A:\MISC_PRG\DPROTECT.COM
      A:\MISC_PRG\DPROTECT.DOC
      A:\MISC_PRG\STRING.COM
      A:\MISC_PRG\UNDEL.COM
      A:\MISC_PRG\UNDEL.DOC
      A:\README.DOC

  362496 bytes total disk space
       0 bytes in 1 hidden files
    5120 bytes in 5 directories
  303104 bytes in 12 user files
   54272 bytes available on disk

  655360 bytes total memory
  591024 bytes free
```

**Fig. M-1.** CHKDSK listing using the /V option.

## Anti-Viral Utility Disk

The disk is divided into five subdirectories; CAWARE, CHKANSI2, FICHECK5, FSP__152, and MISC__PRG. (Incidentally, to type the "__" character, press and hold the Shift key and press the dash "-" key to the right of the "O" key on the top row of the keyboard.) A documentation file named README.DOC is located in the root directory and contains a brief description of the contents and organization of the disk. To view this file, type:

    TYPE A: \README.DOC

then press Return. The pause key can be used to stop the text from scrolling off the top of the screen.

All of the files contained in subdirectories, with the exception of those in the MISC__PRG subdirectory, are stored in a self-extracting archive format. This means that all the various files (executables, documentation, etc.) belonging to a particular program have been compressed and stored as a single file using an archive utility (PKXARC from PKware). Normally, archived files have an ARC extension; however, the archived files on this disk have been modified to be self-extracting so that no archive utility is needed to expand an archived file back into its original form. Thus, because these archived files contain a de-archive program, they have EXE extensions. The self-extracting archive program used to prepare the archived files on this disk is PKSFX, part of the PKXARC archive utility, and has been licensed from PKware for use with this disk. A later section of this manual describes how to extract the archived files.

## DISK CONTENTS

There are three full featured anti-viral software packages, Check ANSI Version 2, File Integrity Checker Version 5.0, and Flu__Shot + Version 1.52, on the enclosed disk. All of these packages are very popular and well respected. The disk also contains an anti-viral utility for C programmers and several other useful utilities. Descriptions of some of the programs can be found in Chapter 4, but the best way to learn about all of the programs is to read their documentation, which is reproduced later in this manual.

## EXTRACTING THE FILES

As covered earlier, the diskette is divided into subdirectories as shown:

| | |
|---|---|
| CAWARE | C Aware for Turbo C |
| CHKANSI2 | Check ANSI |
| FICHECK5 | File Integrity Check |
| FSP__152 | Flu__Shot + Version 1.52 |
| MISC__PRG | Miscellaneous Programs |

The only file in the root directory of the enclosed diskette should be the README.DOC file.

With the exception of the files in the MISC__PRG subdirectory, the programs, documentation, and support files have been stored in a *self-extracting archive format* in order to fit all the files on one 360K disk. For example, all the files needed for Flu__Shot + are archived in the file FSP__152.EXE in the FSP__152 subdirectory, and the same is true for CAWARE, CHKANSI2, and FICHECK5.

To extract the files from their archive format so that you can use them on your computer, you must copy the appropriate EXE file from this diskette to a blank, formatted diskette or a hard drive; there is not enough room on this diskette to extract the files. Next, simply execute the copied self-extracting archive file by typing its filename and pressing Return. After the extraction process is over, you can delete the copied archive EXE file from the disk you copied it to.

For example, assuming that you are using a PC with a 5¼-inch disk drive as Drive A and a hard drive as Drive C, you start extracting Flu__Shot + by creating a subdirectory on Drive C for Flu__Shot +. To create the subdirectory, type:

```
MD C:\FSP
```

then press Return (feel free to name the subdirectory whatever you like). Next, put your copy of the enclosed disk into Drive A. Then copy the file FSP__152.EXE to Drive C as follows:

```
COPY A:\FSP__152/FSP__.EXE C:\FSP /V
```

then press Return.
After the file has copied, change to the FSP subdirectory by typing:

```
CD C:\FSP
```

then press Return. Start the self-extraction process by executing FSP__152.EXE. Type:

```
FSP__152
```

then press Return. The file will now extract itself. When the extraction process is done, you can delete the archive file from Drive C by typing:

ERASE FSP__152.EXE

then press Return.

All of the files needed to use Flu__Shot+ Version 1.52 are not contained on Drive C in the FSP subdirectory. Use the same process to extract the other archived files, each in a separate subdirectory. Finally, copy the files in the MISC__PRG subdirectory of your copy of the enclosed disk to Drive C. However, before doing anything else, stop to read the documentation for the programs thoroughly. These are powerful programs and will take some time to learn, so don't rush.

## DOCUMENTATION

To make using the programs on the enclosed disk as easy as possible, I have reproduced the author's documentation files in this section. This will make things much easier for those of you without printers, as well as allowing you to learn about the programs without having to go through the trouble of extracting and printing the documentation files.

The only program that does not have a documentation file provided by the author is STRING.COM in the MISC__PRG subdirectory. STRING.COM is a handy utility that displays all of the text messages in a specified file. For example, you could use STRING.COM to check for phrases such as "ARF! ARF!" or "Cracked by . . ." in programs that you are thinking of running for the first time.

To use STRING.COM, type STRING, a space, and the filename of the program you wish to check. For example, to view the text contained in a file named GAME.EXE in the subdirectory DOWNLOAD on Drive C, type:

STRING C:\DOWNLOAD\GAME.EXE

then press Return. You can use the Pause key to halt the display if text is scrolling off the top of the screen.

The following information is the documentation that accompanies the utilities included on the companion disk.

94

## C AWARE
**C Aware** ©1988, Gilmore Systems

Gilmore Systems
P.O. Box 3831
Beverly Hills, CA 90212-0831 U.S.A.

Voice (213) 275-8006     Data (213) 276-5263

*Make your Turbo C programs self-aware of themselves!*

Now you can allow your COMPILED Turbo C pgms to check themselves for changes in their CRC or filesize, thus detecting if a virus has modified them.

Viruses have become a problem—altering *.EXE and *.COM files these days. Not just viruses, but hackers who modify shareware programs because they don't like looking at the opening screens.

Well, if you're a programmer using Turbo C, you now have a means of protection. You can make your programs aware of their own CRC and filesize—the 2 most likely things to change in the event of a virus or hacker attack.

Enclosed in this archive is this READ.ME file, MAKAWARE. EXE (exe initializer), EXAMPLE.C (sample source for using the checker), and 6 OBJ's—one for each memory model which you can link with your programs to offer you (or your program) security. These OBJ's contain the function exeaware( ) as follows:

```
exeaware(pgmname)
char *pgmname;
```

RETURNS:     0 - no changes, file unaltered.
             1 - CRC changed, file altered.
             2 - size changed, file altered.
             3 - both CRC and size changed, file altered.

The passed parameter "pgmname" is the name of your running program. For example purposes, you could call the function as follows:

```
main(argc,argv)
int argc;
char **argv;
    {
    extern int exeaware( );
    int result;
    ;
```

```
;
;
result = exeaware(argv[0]);   /* this is how to call the function switch(result)
     {
     case 1:
               printf("CRC changed/n");
               break;
     case 2:
               printf("size changed/n");
               break;
     case 3:
               printf("CRC and size changed/n");
               break;
     case 0:
     default:
               printf("No changes/n");
               break;
     }
     ;
     ;
     ;
     }
```

We've included a source file named "example.c" to demonstrate how this works. It first calls exeaware( ) and proves that nothing has been altered in the file. It then alters itself by adding a single byte to the end of the file and re-calls exeaware( ), proving that the CRC and size of file has changed.

See the "example.c" file for details on compiling and linking.

To use this code, take note of the memory model you're using and link with the appropriate .obj file:

```
exeawart.obj   -  tiny model
exeawarc.obj   -  compact model
exeawars.obj   -  small model
exeawarm.obj  -  medium model
exeawarl.obj   -  large model
exeawarh.obj  -  huge model
```

See the "example.c" file for details on compiling and linking.

It is a two-step process to enable this code:

1. First, you must have a call in your main( ) function to exeaware( ) as shown in the "example.c" source file, and you must link with the appropriate memory model.

2. Second, you must run the program MAKAWARE.EXE against your new "exe" file produced by the linker. Again, refer to the "example.c" file for instructions.

This code offers protection that no external programs can offer. At least now, nobody can accuse YOUR program of containing a virus. Although nothing's perfect, I'm sure some hacker will come up with a way of defeating this code manually, but it would be extremely difficult for a virus to alter or defeat this code.

## Register and Get the Source Code

As with all shareware, try it first. If you like it, send us $10. In return for your $10, we'll send you the source code. You'll receive:

EXEAWARE.C - source code needed to reproduce the exeawar?.objfiles.

MAKAWARE.C - source code needed to reproduce the makaware.exe file.

We're not doing anything fancy here. The source code should also work with the Microsoft C compiler. The OBJ's that you now have should only work with the Turbo C compiler/linker.

If you register for $15 instead of $10, we'll give you 6-months of full access to our "Virus Info" BBS in addition to the source code. Our "Virus Info" BBS deals strictly with the topic of computer viruses. You can download text, source, and programs all pertaining to computer virus prevention and detection. A great way to keep informed of the latest viruses going around.

You can use your Visa/MC to phone in your order today!

*One final note:* If you've obtained this archive from a BBS other than ours and question the integrity of these .obj's or the makaware.exe program within this archive, you can download the CAWARE.ARC file from our BBS to be certain nobody "tinkered" with it. You don't have to be a registered user of our BBS to download this file.

- Chuck Gilmore, Pres.
  Gilmore Systems

## Check ANSI
## CHKANSI2 - version 2.0 ©1988, Gilmore Systems

Gilmore Systems
P.O. Box 3831
Beverly Hills, CA 90212-0831 U.S.A.

Voice (213) 275-8006
Data (213) 276-5263    CIS [71350,1070]

*High Tech Solutions to High Tech Problems*

As some of you already know, we offer virus detection programs. We also run the "Virus Info Palladium" BBS.

Since most of us already know about computer viruses and "trojan horse" programs, we won't discuss them here. We'll just mention that these programs must be executed on your computer in order for them to do their dirty work.

We'd like to share with you, two of the most common misbeliefs about computer damage that our vast number of callers have expressed:

1. Damage can ONLY occur when an infected or trojan program is run.
2. Damage CANNOT occur with data, text, or other non-program files.

*THESE STATEMENTS ARE WRONG!* Although damage is *most likely* to occur by running a program, damage may also occur by *typing a text file* or other display file on your computer screen.

Most people now have the ANSI.SYS device driver installed on their computer systems. You can check if this device driver is installed on your system by checking the file CONFIG.SYS on the root directory of your boot disk. If the CONFIG.SYS file contains a statement something like DEVICE=ANSI.SYS, it is installed on your system.

This ANSI (American National Standards Institute) device driver is required by many programs.

### So, What's the Bottom Line?

Before going into the bottom line, a brief understanding of how the ANSI.SYS device driver works is needed. Basically, you can think of this driver as a sort of TSR (like Borland's Sidekick, for example)—always in memory. But it's not activated by keystrokes —it monitors what's being sent to your display screen. It lets everything pass to the screen except for the one thing it looks for—*escape sequences*. Programs requiring the ANSI driver emit escape sequences to the screen to control such things as color, cursor positioning, screen mode, and other things just as a program emits escape sequences to your printer to activate or deactivate certain features such as print fonts, spacing, underlining, etc.

Since these escape sequences are intercepted by the ANSI driver, they do not show up on the screen—you only see their effects.

## The Danger

The danger lies with the fact that the ANSI device driver also responds to an escape sequence which can *remap* or *redefine* any of your keyboard's keys. Not only is it capable of such nuisance things as turning your "A" key into a "P'" or <F10> key, but it is also capable of redefining *any* key to a complete character string—with carriage return. This means, for example, an escape sequence can be emitted to change your <F1> key to mean "ERASE *.EXE"—and if you press your <F1> key *anytime* after the ANSI driver received the redefine escape sequence, you'll quickly find that all of your executable files in whatever directory you were in at the time are GONE!

## There's More!

As if this isn't scary enough, a program does *not* have to be run in order to remap or redefine any of your keys. *Any text or display file may contain embedded ANSI codes!* All you need to do is type the file out to your screen, and the ANSI driver will intercept all embedded codes, which may contain keyboard redefinition. Simply typing a text or display file onto your screen which contains embedded ANSI codes, is the same thing as a program emitting these ANSI codes. The ANSI driver doesn't care where it came from, all it knows is that it's being sent to the display screen, so it intercepts these codes and acts on them.

## What Can I Do?

To be absolutely safe, you could turn off the ANSI driver by removing the DEVICE = ANSI.SYS from your CONFIG.SYS file and restarting your computer, but then you'd probably find a bunch of unreadable garbage on your screen from some programs or from typing certain text or display files which have legitimate ANSI display sequences in them, but there's a much better way.

## CHKANSI2.EXE

We've developed a program here which we call CHKANSI2.EXE (or just CHKANSI2 for short). Simply execute the program without any parameters, and instructions on its use will appear on your screen. As a brief synopsis of the program, CHKANSI2 goes through every byte of any questionable file you have—whether it's a text, display, data, or any other file—and checks for escape sequences. It prints—in English—any escape sequences it finds and concludes with how many escape sequences it found, and out of those, how many are potentially harmful (those that redefine keys). Since an ANSI display file may contain hundreds or even thousands of escape sequences, see the program instructions (by running the program without parameters) for how to turn off the English display of all escape sequences except for those that redefine keyboard keys.

Use CHKANSI2 whenever you've downloaded any text or display file from a BBS, or obtain same from a "friend." You should use CHKANSI2 to check files *prior* to typing or displaying them on your display screen.

## Operating Environment

CHKANSI2 is a bound executable (also known as FAPI or Family Application), meaning it will execute equally well under the DOS or OS/2 operating environment—whichever you prefer. For IBM and all compatible computers.

## Closing Notes

There is no charge, fee, or consideration for this program. CHKANSI2.EXE may be freely distributed as long as it is not altered, the copyright is not removed, and this documentation file is not altered and accompanies the program. The accompanying file TEST2.TXT must not be modified and must also accompany the distribution.

Keyboard key redefinition via ANSI.SYS is not actually part of the ANSI standard, but is unique to DOS and OS/2 and possibly a few other operating systems.

We've included a text file—TEST2.TXT—in this distribution. This file contains embedded ANSI escape sequences. You may run CHKANSI2 against this file to see how it works. *DO NOT TYPE THIS FILE,* as it contains keyboard redefinitions. Just to make sure you don't type the file, we've put an End-Of-File mark as the first character in the file so that none of your keyboard keys get redefined.

This distribution contains 4 files:

CHKANSI2.EXE
CHKANSI2.DOC
TEST2.TXT
READ.ME

- Chuck Gilmore, Pres.
  Gilmore Systems

---

## FILE INTEGRITY CHECKER
### Fixed Disk "File Integrity Checker"*
**FICHECK version 5.0** © 1988, 1989
**MFICHECK version 5.0** © 1988,1989
**PROVECRC version 1.0** © 1988, 1989

Gilmore Systems
P.O. Box 3831
Beverly Hills, CA 90212-0831

Voice: (213) 275-8006    Data: (213) 276-5263

*Preventive Computer Medicine to help keep your system virus free.*

*All Programs designed and written by Chuck Gilmore
First Printing: June, 1988
Second Printing: July, 1988
Third Printing: August, 1988
Fourth Printing: January, 1989

### Important Notices
**Disclaimer**    FICHECK.EXE/MFICHECK.EXE/PROVECRC.EXE are offered *as is* without warranty of any kind. Gilmore Systems assumes no liability or responsibility for loss of profit, data, or any consequential or inconsequential damages resulting from the use

or misuse of these programs. This applies to all versions of the above mentioned programs.

**FICHECK and MFICHECK are Evaluation versions**     Do not attempt to run FICHECK.EXE or MFICHECK.EXE without first reading this document in its entirety!

FICHECK.EXE and MFICHECK.EXE are to serve as evaluation versions only. If you use these evaluation versions for a trial period of time (30 days), we urge you to order one of the commercial versions (see order form at end of this document).

The commercial versions (XFICHECK or PFICHECK) offers advanced, sophisticated state-of-the-art capabilities. But don't just take our word for it, use the supplied evaluation versions to know what kind of quality you can expect. For more information on the commercial versions, see the pages of this document describing XFICHECK / PFICHECK.

**Attention**     FICHECK/MFICHECK are protected by federal copyright laws. We do grant you the right, however to distribute and use these evaluation versions as long as the following criteria are met:

1. The supplied programs and documentation are to be distributed as a group consisting of the following: FICHECK.EXE, MFICHECK.EXE, PROVECRC.EXE, PROVE.BAT, FICHECK5.DOC, and READ.ME files. They are *not* to be unbundled.

2. No modifications, disassemblies, alterations, removal of copyrights or other alterations are to be made, and no additional files are to be added to the above six files.

3. No fee or monetary consideration is to be charged. Diskette copying/distribution services may not charge more than $5.

4. The six files that comprise this evaluation package (as described in number 1 above), are *not* to be bundled, included, or used with any other product(s) or service(s).

5. You *cannot* charge fees to evaluate disk drives with this product.

6. A 30-day trial period is granted. Afterward, you may either order one of the commercial versions or destroy the evaluation copies.

## Introduction

Computer viruses have now become an international concern. They've infected places such as NASA, EDS (subsidiary of GM), universities such as Lehigh university, Miami university, the ARPANET network, and countless other firms as well as individuals. Major software houses are not immune either. If they admit being struck by a virus, nobody would buy their software. You know things are getting bad when you buy a name brand software package at a computer store and find that it's infected by a virus!

## Just What Is a Computer Virus

A computer virus is a small piece of code contained within a seemingly innocent program. What's unique about the code is that when the program is run, it attaches itself to other programs. When those other programs are run, the virus inside them seeks out and attaches itself to yet more programs on your disks. These other programs (the targets) can be *any* program including your operating system (ie: COMMAND.COM). Depending on what instructions are present within the viral code, the results can be quite severe —anything from wiping out your entire fixed disk to ruining your data to altering video I/O functions so that your CRT explodes! These catastrophic results are usually not carried out right away. The people writing these viruses usually set "time bombs" in the viral code. These "time bombs" can be anything—when a certain date is reached; or a certain memory location is written to with a certain value; or the number of files on your disk reaches a certain number; or you run a program a certain number of times—these are just a few examples of "triggers" that viruses set and look for. When the "trigger" happens, then the viral code does its catastrophic dirty work.

## Bulletin Board Systems

In addition to spreading computer viruses by infected software houses, Bulletin Board Systems are a major target for the people who derive pleasure out of writing viral code. *Any* program on a BBS can be downloaded by *anyone*. The person downloading a program from a BBS may be a "virus implanter" and implant the downloaded program with a virus, then upload it to other BBS's where perhaps thousands of people will download the infected

tions and as a result, some companies have banned the downloading of programs from BBS's. This is indeed a shame, since BBS's are there for the sharing of knowledge, information, and the opportunity to get talented programmer's works known.

## How Can I Tell If My
## Computer Has Infected Programs?

Simply put, you *cannot*! That's the scariest part of it all. Viruses may lie dormant for months or years on an infected system before they show their symptoms. Programs will continue to run normally until one day when the "trigger" is reached.

## What Can I Do to Stop a Potential Virus?

There are some viral-fighting programs available such as FLU-SHOT, and versions of VACCINE. These programs attempt to block viruses from doing things that viruses typically do. They attempt to block any altering of COMMAND.COM or your other operating system's system files. They try to alert you of low-level disk writing. These programs look for other things as well, but may slow your system down as a result. Some require you to make lists of approved programs and TSR's. The problem with these programs are that they are running on your system which may contain a virus that looks for these particular programs and renders them inactive or makes them think that everything's ok (sounds like AIDs, doesn't it?) while they do their dirty work. The original version of FLU-SHOT was found to contain a virus itself (NOT from the original author), although newer versions have been corrected. Because of this, we urge you to download virus detection programs from the BBS's of their original authors (ie: Gilmore Systems' BBS for FICHECK, Ross Greenberg's BBS for FluShot, etc).

## Introducing FICHECK / MFICHECK

FICHECK and MFICHECK are programs which differ from vaccine-type programs and other programs that attempt to find, block, or alert you to viruses. FICHECK does none of these things. As a matter of fact, FICHECK can't even be run from your fixed disk! FICHECK is a preventive medicine program which sort of takes a snapshot (x-ray) of your entire fixed disk(s) and logs it to a file. The things FICHECK logs are the date, time, size, attribute, and CRC

(Cyclic Redundancy Check) of every file on your fixed disk(s). It looks for differences in all of these things whenever you decide to run it again and alerts you to any changes. Any changes potentially mean a virus is at work—viruses have to alter files in some way in order to spread themselves. MFICHECK does the same thing as FICHECK except it uses our unique MCRC (Modified Cyclic Redundancy Check) instead of standard CRC checking.

FICHECK also checks the CRC of your master boot record/partition table (MFICHECK checks the MCRC of your master boot record/partition table) and logs this information as well as available disk space and FAT (File Allocation Table) ID byte. When these programs compare your actual disk information against the log (boot record info, FAT ID byte, disk space, all file parameters: date, time, size, attribute, CRC or MCRC), any discrepencies are reported to you, suggesting a possible virus at work—especially if the master boot record/partition table info has been changed.

FICHECK and MFICHECK can also optionally check your system's interrupt vectors for changes. Because of the nature of how FICHECK and MFICHECK work, you'll quickly find that they double as a complete file tracking system. In essence, these programs serve a dual purpose.

## CRC Checking vs MCRC Checking

CRC (Cyclic Redundancy Check) is a sophisticated check of sequential bytes in a file resulting in a unique number for that file. This unique number should change in the event any one or more bytes of the file change. If the CRC number for the file changes, it indicates the file has changed.

CRC has been around for many years in communications protocols for transferring files from one computer to another over telephone lines with modems. When sending files across telephone lines, CRC checking does its job very well to ensure that the data the receiving computer gets matches the data the sending computer sends.

CRC was designed specifically for communications between computers. However, CRC *is not a reliable method for detecting changes to files that already exist on your disk system!* Later in this document, we'll prove that to you with a program that will alter a file and keep its CRC intact.

Basically, a resident virus on your system has all day to modify your files and keep the original CRC of those files the same. So-called anti-viral or file checking programs claiming to alert you of changes to your files based solely on CRC checking will offer no protection against virus or trojan programs capable of file alteration while maintaining CRC integrity.

MCRC is a unique, modified CRC check developed exclusively by us at Gilmore Systems for the sole purpose of checking files on your disk system for modification. Our MCRC check is a highly reliable, state of the art check used in determining changes to files on your disk system.

While CRC can be fooled by clever viruses and trojans, MCRC does NOT fall victim to these file altering programs. MCRC will detect changes to files where CRC shows no change.

You may be asking yourself at this point - what if some hacker tears apart our code and discovers our MCRC algorithm, then incorporates a means of modifying files in his virus programs which leave MCRC intact? This is an excellent question but rest assured that if this happens, standard CRC checking will show the change. In other words, one or the other of CRC or MCRC (but not both) will change with an altered file.

As promised earlier, here's how to work the PROVECRC.EXE program which will prove to you that file alteration is possible without affecting the original CRC.

**Important**    Before you try this example, read the rest of this user's manual completely, then come back to this example!

First, choose a file between 25 and 32,000 bytes in length to be altered (if you can't think of any, use our PROVECRC.EXE program as the file itself). Next, enter the following on the DOS command line:

    PROVECRC  INFILE  OUTFILE

where *INFILE* is the name of the file to alter, and *OUTFILE* is the name of the file to store the altered copy in. *INFILE* will remain intact, but *OUTFILE* will have an altered copy of *INFILE* which retains the same CRC as *INFILE* and the same date, time, size, and attributes. Next, run a CRC checking program (or use FICHECK.EXE as described later in this document with the "/s = " option) to show the CRC of *INFILE* and *OUTFILE*, noting that the CRC values of each file are identical. Repeat this process with MFICHECK.EXE, noting the different MCRC values for each file. You can also run the DOS COMP program to prove that the two files are indeed different!

The above process can be automated with the PROVE.BAT file provided. Simply enter the following on the DOS command line:

Prove *INFILE OUTFILE*

**Important Note**  Throughout the remainder of this document we will use FICHECK to mean either FICHECK.EXE or MFICHECK.EXE. Both are identical except FICHECK does CRC checking, and MFICHECK does MCRC checking. We use the terms *hard disk* and *fixed disk* interchangeably.

## Using FICHECK / MFICHECK

You should have the following programs/files on your disk:

| | |
|---|---|
| FICHECK5.DOC | This document |
| FICHECK.EXE | The FICHECK version 5.0 program |
| MFICHECK.EXE | The MFICHECK version 5.0 program |
| PROVECRC.EXE | The CRC disprover program |
| PROVE.BAT | Batch file for PROVECRC.EXE |
| READ.ME | Text of announcements, changes, etc. |

If you've used previous versions of FICHECK/MFICHECK, please destroy and replace them with these newer versions. These newer versions (version 5.0) are upward compatible with the logs created by version 4.x (but not versions lower than 4.0).

FICHECK should *not* be placed on your fixed disk. It will *only run from a floppy disk* , and furthermore, *DOS must be booted from that floppy disk!*

Why all the hassle of booting from and running from a floppy disk? Simple. If you boot from a fixed disk, you may be booting from an infected copy of your operating system, starting an infected TSR, have an infected device driver, or may have run an infected program. If you boot from a floppy disk, you don't give the viruses on your fixed disk a chance to become active. Therefore, the first thing you should do in order to prepare for using the FICHECK program is:

1. Boot DOS from your ORIGINAL distribution disk.
2. Format a bootable floppy disk. (use the command FORMAT A:/S)
3. Copy FICHECK.EXE to the newly formatted disk.

4. Diskcopy this new disk for as many fixed disk drives or logical drives you have on your system and label each one for a specific drive (ie: FICHECK for Drive C:, FICHECK for Drive D:, etc).

Anytime you want to run FICHECK, you should first *turn your computer off*, then back on with the bootable FICHECK diskette in Drive A: (Hitting Ctrl-Alt-Del may not get rid of actively running viruses).

FICHECK can be run either way: 1) interactively or 2) using command line arguments.

## Running FICHECK Interactively

Simply type and enter FICHECK on the command line. You'll be presented with a screen containing three sets of fields to fill in:

1. The Drive Letter of the fixed disk you wish to check.

2. The Processing Option you wish FICHECK to perform.

3. The filename extensions of the files you wish to check.

The first field simply asks for the drive letter of the fixed disk drive you wish to check.

The second field has one of three answers: N, C, or P which stand for New, Check, and Print, respectively. The first time you run FICHECK you should choose N which will scan your fixed disk and log a "snapshot" of your files, master boot record/partition table, FAT (File Allocation Table) ID byte, disk free space, and interrupt vectors. FICHECK will create two log files on floppy Drive A named DRIVEx.CCK (holding file information), and DRIVEx.CDI (holding boot record and space information) where the "x" is the drive letter of the drive that's being logged. (Note that MFICHECK uses extensions of .MCK and .MDI instead). You should run FICHECK with the N option after every BACKUP or immediately before running a new program, or whenever appropriate. Using the N option logs all files which may have been added since the last time you used the N option.

Choosing C or P requires that your printer be turned on (writes to LPT1 or PRN). After running N, you should rerun the program choosing P for a readable hardcopy of the log (P runs at lightning speed).

Run FICHECK with the C option after anytime you've run a new program such as one that may have been downloaded from a BBS (or even purchased from a store). Besides after running a new program, it would be very beneficial to give your disk a weekly checkup by running FICHECK with the C option. FICHECK will print any discrepencies in checks of the actual files on your fixed disk against the log entries, as well as report on any deleted or added files, and any removed or added directories, changed volume names, changed master boot record/partition table info, FAT ID byte, disk free space, and optionally-changed interrupt vectors. This report should alert you to possible infection by viruses present on your system and which files or programs may have become infected. Some discrepencies are normal:

- If you're a programmer, the only EXE, COM, OBJ, LIB, SYS or BAT files that should have changed are the ones YOU create or modify.

- If you've edited an existing text file, this will be reported by FICHECK if you've used "*" or supplied its extension.

- Many programs modify data files (ie: database programs modify database files, games may modify their own data files, etc). This is normal but will be reported by FICHECK nonetheless.

- If you've asked for the Interrupt Vector report, some changes to interrupts are normal—consult with an experienced technical programmer about any reported changes.

The third field lets you enter anywhere from 0 to 10 different extensions (filename extensions) which can be anywhere from one to three characters including the wildcards (? and *). If you're not familiar with wildcards, please consult your DOS manual. Whenever you specify extensions, FICHECK only looks for and checks filenames on your fixed disk that match the extensions you supply. For instance, if you supply EXE, COM, SYS, and BAT (which we recommend as a minimum), FICHECK will only check or look for files matching those extensions (ie: .EXE, .COM, .SYS, and .BAT). Some programs use overlays, usually matching the OV? extension. For maximum protection, use * by itself to check and look for *every* file on your fixed disk (including those without any extensions). If you use "*" (without quotes) by itself, *all* files on your fixed disk will be specified, whereas if you use * as in XX*, all files matching XX* will be specified along with any other extensions you specify (if any). If you don't enter any extensions, * will default (ALL files). NOTE: *We very strongly suggest using * every time you use "FICHECK"—no matter which option (N,C,P) you choose.*

Once all three fields have been filled in by you, press the F2 key on your keyboard to start processing. Anytime before pressing F2, you can press F1 for brief help with the field you're on, or F10 to quit the program.

## Running FICHECK With Command Line Arguments

You can run FICHECK with command line arguments in one of three methods:

| method 1 | FICHECK | d: | /n = EXT | /c = EXT | /p = EXT |
| | | | [/o = OUTFILE] | | |
| method 2 | FICHECK | /s = FILESPEC | | | |
| method 3 | FICHECK | /v | | | |

**Method 1**    The arguments are not case sensitive so feel free to use lower and/or uppercase characters. Spacing is not important either, use spaces wherever you want or none at all. The argument definitions are:

| | |
|---|---|
| d: | The drive letter of the fixed disk drive to check. |
| /n = | Identical to N of field 2 of interactive usage. |
| /c = | Identical to C of field 2 of interactive usage. |
| /p = | Identical to P of field 2 of interactive usage. |
| EXT | Identical to field 3 of interactive usage. Extensions must be separated by commas. |
| [/o = OUTFILE] | The brackets surrounding this argument mean it's optional—don't use the brackets. /o = OUTFILE, if present, will print output to the filespec specified by OUTFILE instead of your printer. OUTFILE should contain a COMPLETE PATH INCLUDING DRIVE. Note that printed output (which would be routed to OUTFILE) takes place when the C or P options are used. |

Note that ONLY ONE of /n = , /c = , or /p = is to be used (just as in the interactive mode). Examples:

| | |
|---|---|
| FICHECK c: /n = * | creates new log of ALL files on Drive C. |
| FICHECK c: /n = exe,com,sys,bat | creates new log of files on Drive C: matching *.exe, *.com, *.sys, *.bat |
| FICHECK e:/p = * | makes a readable hardcopy of everything in the DRIVEE.CCK log. Also useful for a great "enhanced" disk drive listing. |
| FICHECK e:/p = *  /o = c: \ log_e | same as above but creates file C: \ LOG_E and prints to this file instead of your printer. |
| FICHECK f:/c = * | checks Drive F against the log DRIVEF.CCK and prints any discrepencies on your printer. |
| FICHECK f:  /c = *  /o = c: \ report | same as above but creates file C: \ REPORT and prints to this file instead of your printer. |
| FICHECK d:  /c = exe,com,sys,bat | checks Drive D against log DRIVED.CCK and prints any discrepencies on your printer. Note that only *.exe, *.com, *.sys, and *.bat will be checked against the matching log entries. |

**Method 2**    FICHECK / MFICHECK has the ability to scan single files (or groups of files via wildcards) for CRC calculation (or MCRC calculation with MFICHECK). This feature is invoked by using the "/s = " option. Note that when "/s = " is used, no other command line arguments are allowed. Also note that when "/s = " is used, you are not limited to hard disks—you may specify floppy drives. When "/s = " is used, the file(s) will be listed along with their size, date, time, attribute, and CRC or MCRC. Examples:

| | |
|---|---|
| FICHECK   /s = *.exe | calculates and displays info on *.exe files in current directory. |
| FICHECK   /s = c: \ ibmbio.com | calculates and displays info about c: \ ibmbio.com. |
| FICHECK   /s = a: \ *.bat | calculates and displays info about all *.bat files found in current directory for Drive A. |

111

FICHECK  /s = *.*  > prn        calculates and prints info (on printer)
                                about all files in current directory and
                                drive.

*Note:* Logs are not used, created, read, or modified when the "/s = "
option is used. Also note that the "/s = " option is only
available during command line processing and that no other
options are allowed when "/s = " is used.

**Method 3**    FICHECK incorporates code that can test itself to see
if any changes to itself were made. To test the validity of FICHECK,
simply enter:

FICHECK  /v

FICHECK will then perform a validity test of itself. You should use
this method periodically to insure that FICHECK has not become
infected or altered in any way.

## Changing the FICHECK / MFICHECK
## screen appearance

The FICHECK screen was designed with color monitors in
mind. Although FICHECK incorporates code to automatically detect
your monitor type (color or monochrome), you can force changes
to the screen appearance by use of an environment variable. To do
this, enter one of the following on the DOS command line prior to
starting FICHECK (you only need to do this once unless you restart
your machine):

SET SCRMODE = MONO
SET SCRMODE = OTHER

If you have a color monitor and don't like the blue background, you
would use the SET SCRMODE = MONO command above. If you have
a nonstandard monitor and the FICHECK screen doesn't display
properly, use the SET SCRMODE = OTHER command above. To turn
off these commands (defaulting back to the built-in auto-detection),
enter SET SCRMODE = .

## Reporting/Checking Interrupt Vectors

In addition to changing the screen appearance above, there is
1 additional environment setting which you can use with FICHECK:

```
SET INTREPORT = YES
SET INTREPORT = NO
```

Although FICHECK logs interrupt vectors during the N (new) option, it will not print or check them during P (print) or C (check) options unless you set the above environment variable to YES.

## More Information

Even if you only plan on using FICHECK / MFICHECK in the interactive mode of operation, you should still view the help screens by entering one of the following on the DOS command line:

```
FICHECK    /help
MFICHECK   /help
```

There are 4 screens of help which will present themselves. The last screen also provides information on our commercial XFICHECK (eXtended FICHECK) and our PFICHECK (Professional FICHECK).

## Important Final Remarks

Whenever booting your system from a floppy disk, it is extremely important to boot from the same version of DOS on floppy disk as that on your fixed disk!

Running FICHECK with the N option will only log the current state of your files on your fixed disk(s), which may already contain infected files. Subsequent runs using the C option alert you to any changes which may have occurred. Any of the changes reported is an alert of a potential virus. If a file has changed that shouldn't have, remove it from your system immediately and replace it with the same file from your original distribution diskette. If COMMAND. COM, IBMBIO.COM, or IBMDOS.COM have changed on your Drive C, turn off your computer immediately. Insert your original DOS diskette in Drive A and restart your computer. Once restarted, do a SYS C: to overwrite these files to the way they should be. If COMMAND.COM was the only file that changed, turn off your computer immediately. Insert your original DOS diskette in Drive A and restart your computer. Once restarted, do a COPY COMMAND.COM C: or to the appropriate disk drive.

FICHECK searches all file attributes—system, hidden, etc. Once processing has started, FICHECK starts a timer and when processing finishes, FICHECK prints how long it ran. On computers running at 4.77 MHz such as the original IBM XT's, FICHECK may take a while to complete its job. On computers such as the IBM PS/2 Model 80 running at 20 MHz, FICHECK flies right through. We've incorporated fast algorithms so that FICHECK will run through your system as fast as possible.

It's pretty difficult to evade a CRC (Cyclic Redundancy Check) of your files, not to mention changing file size by adding a couple of bytes or so.

Clever viruses install themselves over unused portions of program files, and manage to keep the same size, date, time, and attribute of the file.

But even with these protective checks, CRC does not guarantee that some clever deviant may code a virus to attempt to match the original CRC of a file it altered. There are no reports of this yet, but as more CRC checking programs such as this are in use, virus-writing programmers will have to incorporate code (mutations) to match the CRC of the original file when they alter it. It's not a small task for them, however, CRC checking is a well known method. If you can test a file for CRC, you can alter a file such that its CRC stays the same. Because of this, we offer another version of FICHECK (MFICHECK or Modified FICHECK) which uses a unique, modified CRC check which is not known to the virus-writing programmers (and we won't make the method public in order to protect you). Since the modification we made to the CRC algorithm is unknown to anyone but us, a virus-writing programmer will not know how to defeat the check. The MFICHECK program is distributed with FICHECK, and its operation is identical to that of FICHECK with 2 exceptions: 1) it uses an extension of .MCK and .MDI instead of .CCK and .CDI, and 2) it uses our unique Modified CRC (MCRC) check instead of standard CRC checking.

We also anticipate these deviant virus-writing programmers to hack away at our MFICHECK program in an attempt to discover the MCRC checking algorithm so that the viruses they write can also modify your programs and files to match our MCRC values. Have no fear—we have a solution to that too. Although its possible for a virus to alter the contents of a file and cleverly maintain the same CRC value, the MCRC value will change. Likewise, if the virus incorporates code that alters a file and cleverly maintains the same MCRC, the CRC value will change. No matter what the virus does to your files, if it is altered in any way, either the CRC or the MCRC has to change. It is virtually impossible to alter a file and maintain both the original CRC and MCRC values—one or the other will change and will be detected by our File Integrity Checking programs. You could employ this dual checking method by running FICHECK, then immediately running MFICHECK but that would be too time consuming to be worth the bother—we have another solution—read on!

Our commercial XFICHECK (eXtended FICHECK) for $15, incorporates both CRC and MCRC checking in a single pass, and doesn't take much longer to run than MFICHECK. The added security and peace of mind of dual-checking for CRC and MCRC alone is worth the price, but that's not all XFICHECK does. XFICHECK does everything FICHECK and MFICHECK does together, and has more features:

- Dual CRC and MCRC checking in a single pass! Saves enormous time! Can optionally be forced to do CRC or MCRC only.

- Allows exclusion of extensions from searches as well as inclusion (saves more time!)

- Can optionally ignore the archive bit of the attribute byte (eliminates long reports when C option is used after a backup is performed).

- Records information on *all* bootable partitions (FICHECK only does the master boot record/partition table).

- Stores actual master boot record/partition table and *all* separate boot partitions on disk—saves this in a hidden/read-only file on floppy disk.

- Can optionally restore master boot record/partition table and any of the separate boot partitions.

- Can optionally be run from hard disk (without boot from floppy disk and without starting the program from floppy disk—*NOT RECOMMENDED).*

- Reports on disk space also include: available clusters, total clusters, bytes per sector, and sectors per cluster as well as any changes to them. This is in addition to disk free space and FAT ID.

- Can be run from the command line to do a quick CRC and MCRC of any file or group of files on any disk (including floppy disks). Does not require or use the log.

- Reports all files within new directories (those not logged).

- Shows before and after values of any changed interrupt vectors.
- Stores information in the log as to its creation criteria:
  - ☐ search extensions specified in creation
  - ☐ search extensions excluded in creation
  - ☐ date/time of log creation (independent of date/time of file)
- Log creation criteria (above) is printed in all reports along with:
  - ☐ search extensions specified for current report
  - ☐ search extensions excluded for current report
  - ☐ date/time of current report

PFICHECK (Professional FICHECK) for $20, has all of the above features of XFICHECK but is geared more for the corporate or other user who needs more computing power and flexibility:

- Update feature can create new logs during the C (checking) process.
- Can override floppy logs, and read/write/process logs on hard disk.
- Sophisticated ERRORLEVEL return for batch processing.
- Can run on Local Area Networks (LANs)—won't abort if it can't open a file that's in use.

## Order Today!

If you've obtained this copy of FICHECK from a friend or BBS (shared programs), there is *NO* guarantee that your copy of FICHECK hasn't become infected by a virus. We cannot guarantee that somebody didn't download this program, infect it (purposely or accidentally), and pass it on by uploading it to other BBS's or giving it to friends. If there's any question about integrity, download FICHECK5.ARC from our BBS.

Once you've tried FICHECK/MFICHECK for 30 days and are satisfied, order one of our commercial versions (see last page of document for order info).

Unless you specifically request a 3½-inch micro-floppy disk, we will send you a 5¼-inch floppy disk. FICHECK, MFICHECK, XFICHECK and PFICHECK will run on all true IBM compatible computers running the IBM PC-DOS or MS-DOS operating systems versions 2.0 and above. Some fixed disks require drivers which should be placed on your boot diskettes from the original driver distribution diskette. FICHECK, MFICHECK, XFICHECK and PFICHECK will run on the entire family of IBM (and compatible) computers ranging from the XT to all of the PS/2 models. Fixed disks containing the OS/2 operating system and associated files can also be checked since they maintain the same file structure as DOS—you must still format DOS bootable diskettes to use the programs.

To order, send $15 for XFICHECK (Calif. residents add .98 sales tax), or $20 for PFICHECK (Calif. residents add 1.30 sales tax) to:

Gilmore Systems
P.O. Box 3831
Beverly Hills, CA 90212-0831

or call us with your VISA/MC number at (213) 275-8006—or use your Visa/MC online (our ''Virus Info'' BBS) at (213) 276-5263.

**Bonus!**   As a bonus for ordering, we will grant you 6-months of usage on the ''Virus Info'' section of our BBS which deals with the topic of Computer Viruses. The ''Virus Info'' file section has text files, programs, source code and news articles ready for downloading. The ''Virus Info'' file section is only visible and available to those who've purchased our commercial XFICHECK or PFICHECK programs. All other sections are available to all callers—so give our BBS a call and browse around—download the file that lists all files on the board (includes list of files in the ''Virus Info'' file section). Public message section is also available.

Many companies such as us use BBS systems to exchange and share information, ideas, new technologies, programs, tools, and multitudes of other things. How can you continue to use these invaluable offerings in fear of destruction of your most valuable programs, data, or even hardware? We hope that our ''File Integrity Check'' programs will offer you security against these fears and at the same time inspire other programmers to create other anti-viral or preventive computer medicine type programs.

- Chuck Gilmore, Pres.
  Gilmore Systems

```
XFICHECK / PFICHECK Order Form
                    Please Print Clearly


Your Name: _____

Shipping Address: _____

                   _____

                   _____

Phone Number: (_____) _____-_____

How did you hear of us? _____

                        _____

Check Diskette Type: ____ 5.25" diskette     ____ 3.5" diskette

Computer Type: _____

___ Professional File Integrity Checker @ $20 ea (PFICHECK) - _____.____
              If in California, add $1.30 ea sales tax - _____.____

___       eXtended File Integrity Checker @ $15 ea (XFICHECK) - _____.____
              If in California, add $0.98 ea sales tax - _____.____

 Each Order includes 6 mos BBS access. Add $5 ea for 12 mos - _____.____

                                          Total: _____.____

We pay shipping/handling. Enclose payment in U.S. funds, or charge to:

VISA or MC # _____-_____-_____-_____   Expiration: ___/___

Name (EXACTLY as on Credit Card): _____

Today's Date __/__/__ Signature: _____
                      Send to:

                   Gilmore Systems
                   P.O. BOX 3831
              Beverly Hills, Calif. 90212-0831
                      U.S.A.

   Contact us (voice) at (213) 275-8006 for: - Site Licensing Info
                                             - Dealer Inquiries
                                             - Quantity Discounts
                                             - Faster Credit Card Orders

Credit card purchasers can also order online on our BBS at (213)276-5263


    FICHECK/MFICHECK User Guide - (C)Copyright 1988,89, Gilmore Systems
```

## FLU_SHOT+

## FLU_SHOT+™ version 1.5

Ross M. Greenberg
Software Concepts Design
594 Third Avenue
New York, New York 10016

BBS: (212) 889-6438    1200|2400|N/8/1

*A Form of Protection from Viral and Trojan Programs*

Not for Commercial Distribution without written permission by the copyright holder. Noncommercial copying of this software and this documentation is encouraged. Commercial Distribution is easily defined: if you distribute this software, or the enclosed documentation, for more than your cost of such distribution, then you're a Commercial Distributor and require our written permission. Not-for-profit organizations and computer user groups, and their bulletin board systems (if any) are specifically *not* considered commercial distributors.

By your using this software, you agree to the terms herein. Specifically, that you do not have the right to copy this software except as outlined above, and that you are granted a license to use this software only by registering this software as mentioned elsewhere in this document.

You also agree, and signify that agreement by using this software, that Software Concepts Design and Ross M. Greenberg will not be held liable for any reason for any cost you may incur, or any potential income you might lose as a result of using this software. Finally, this software is provided "AS IS," meaning that what you see is what you get. If you use this software and a tree falls on your house, or your spouse leaves you for someone younger and more virile, please do not bother having your lawyer call—it isn't the fault of the software, no matter what the lawyer tries to convince you!

## What is a Trojan?

Back in the good old days (before there were computers), there was this bunch of soldiers who had no chance of beating a superior force or of even making it into their fortress. They had this nifty idea: present the other side with a gift. Once the gift had been accepted, soldiers hiding within the gift would sneak out and overtake the enemy from within.

We can only think of the intellectual giants of the day who would accept a gift large enough to house enemy soldiers without checking its contents. Obviously, they had little opportunity to watch old WWII movies to see the same device used over and over again. They probably wouldn't have appreciated Hogan's Heroes anyway. No color TV's—or at least not ones with reliable reception.

Consider the types of people who would be thrilled at the concept of owning their own rough hewn, large wooden horse! Perhaps they wanted to be the first one on their block, or something silly like that.

Anyway, you're all aware of the story of The Trojan Horse.

Bringing ourselves a bit closer to the reality we've all grown to know and love, there's a modern day equivalent: getting a gift from your BBS or user group which contains a little gem which will attack your hard disk, destroying whatever data it contains.

In order to understand how a potentially useful program can cause such damage when corrupted by some misguided soul, it's useful to understand how your disk works, and how absurdly easy it is to cause damage to the data contained thereon. So, a brief technical discussion of the operation of your disk is in order. For those who aren't concerned, turn the page or something.

Data is preserved on a disk in a variety of different physical ways having to do with how the data is encoding in the actual recording of that data. The actual *structure* of that data, however, is the same between MS-DOS machines. Other operating systems have a different structure, but that doesn't concern us now.

Each disk has a number of "tracks." These are sometimes called cylinders from the old type IBMer's. These are the same people who call hard disks DASDs (Direct Access Storage Devices), so we can safely ignore their techno-speak, and just call them tracks. Tracks can be thought of as the individual little grooves on an audio record, sort of.

Anyway, each track is subdivided into a number of sectors. Each track has the same number of sectors. Tracks are numbered, as are sectors. Any given area on the disk can be accessed if a request is made to read or write data into or out of Track-X, Sector Y. The read or write command is given to the disk controller, which is an interface between the computer itself and the hard disk. The controller figures out what commands to send to the hard disk, the hard disk responds and the data is read or written as directed.

The first track on the hard disk typically will contain a small program which is read from the hard disk and executed when you first power up your machine. The power up sequence is called "booting" your machine, and therefore the first track is typically known as the "boot track."

In order to read information from your disk in a logical sequence, there has to be some sort of index. An unusual index method was selected for MS-DOS. Imagine going to the card index in a library, looking up the title you desire, and getting a place in another index which tells you where on the racks the book is stored. Now, when you read the book, you discover that only the first chapter of the book is there. In order to find the next chapter of the book, you have to go back to that middle index, which tells you where the next chapter is stored. This process continues until you get to the end of the book. Sounds pretty convoluted, right? You bet! However, this is pretty much how MS-DOS does its "cataloguing" of files.

The directory structure of MS-DOS allows for you to look up an item called the "first cluster." A cluster represents a set of contiguous ("touching or in contact" according to Random House) tracks and sectors. It is the smallest amount of information which the file structure of MS-DOS knows how to read or write.

Based on the first cluster number as stored in the directory, the first portion of a file can be read. When the information contained therein is exhausted, MS-DOS goes to that secondary index for a pointer to the next cluster. That index is called the *File Allocation Table*, commonly abbreviated to "FAT." The FAT contains an entry for each cluster on the disk. A FAT entry can have a few values: ones which indicate that the cluster is unused; another which indicates that the associated cluster has been damaged somehow and that it should be marked as a "bad cluster"; and a pointer to the next cluster for a given file. This allows for what is called a *linked list*: once you start looking up clusters associated with a given file, each FAT entry tells you what the next cluster is. At the end of the linked list is a special indicator which indicates that there are no more clusters associated with the file.

There are actually two copies of the FAT stored on your disk, but no one really knows what the second copy was intended for. Often, if the first copy of the FAT is corrupted for some reason, a clever programmer could recover information from the second copy to restore to the primary FAT. These clever programmers can be called "hackers," and should not be confused with the thieves who break into computer systems and steal things, or the "worms" [Joanne Dow gets credit for *that* phrase!] who would get joy out of causing you heartache!

But that heartache is exactly what can happen if the directory (which contains the pointer to the first cluster a file uses), the FAT (which contains that linked list to other areas on the disk which the file uses), or other areas of the disk get corrupted.

And that's what the little "worms" who create Trojan programs do: they cause what at first appears to be a useful program to eventually corrupt the important parts of your disk. This can be as simple as changing a few bytes of data, or can include wiping entire tracks clean.

Not all programs which write to your hard disk are bad ones, obviously. Your word processor, spreadsheet, database and utility programs have to write to the hard disk. Some of the DOS programs (such as FORMAT), if used improperly, can also erase portions of your hard disk causing you massive amounts of grief. You'd be surprised what damage the simple "DEL" command can do with just a simple typo.

But, what defines a Trojan program is its delivery mechanism: the fact that you're running something you didn't expect. Typical Trojan programs cause damage to your data, and were designed to do so by the "worms" who writhe in delight at causing this damage. May they rot in hell—a mind is a terrible thing to waste!

Considering the personality required to cause such damage, you can rest assured that they have few friends, and even their mother doesn't like to be in the same room with them. They sit back and chortle about the damage they do with a few other lowly "worms." This is their entire social universe. You should pity them. I know that I do.

## What is a Virus?

Trojan programs are but a delivery mechanism, as stated above. They can be implemented in a clever manner, so that they only trigger the malicious part on a certain date, when your disk contains certain information or whatever. However they're coded, though, they typically affect the disk only in a destructive manner once triggered.

A new breed of programs has the capability of not only reserving malicious damage for a given event's occurrence, but of also replicating itself as well. This is what people refer to when they mention the term "Virus Program."

Typically, a virus will spread itself by replicating a portion of itself onto another program. Later, when that normally safe program is run it will, in part, execute a set of instructions which will infect other programs and then potentially, trigger the Trojan portion of the program contained within the virus.

The danger of the virus program is twofold. First, it contains a Trojan which will cause damage to your hard disk. The second danger is the reason why everyone is busy building bomb shelters. This danger is that the virus program will infect other programs and they in turn will infect other programs and so forth. Since it can also infect programs on your floppy disks, you could unknowingly infect other machines! Pretty dangerous stuff, alright!

Kenneth van Wyck, one of the computer folks over at Lehigh University, first brought a particular virus to the attention of the computer community. This virus infects a program, which every MS-DOS computer must have, called COMMAND.COM. This is the Command Line Interpreter and is the interface between your keyboard and the MS-DOS operating system itself. Whatever you type at the C> prompt will be interpreted by it.

Well, the virus subverts this intended function, causing the infection of neighboring COMMAND.COMs before continuing with normal functionality of the command you typed. After a certain number of "infections," the Trojan aspect of the program goes off, causing you to lose data.

The programmer was clever. But still a "worm". And still deserving of contempt instead of respect. Think of what good purposes the programmer could have put his or her talents to instead of creating this damage. And consider what this programmer must do, in covering up what they've done. They certainly can't tell anyone what they've accomplished. Justifiable homicide comes to mind, but since the "worms" they must hang around are probably as disreputable as they are, they must hold their little creation a secret.

A pity. Hopefully, the "worm" is losing sleep. Or getting a sore neck looking behind them wondering which of their "friends" is gonna turn them in for the reward I list towards the end of this document.

## The Challenge to the "Worm"

When I first released a program to try to thwart their demented little efforts, I published this letter in the archive (still in the FLU_SHOT + archive of which this is a part). What I say in it still holds:

> As for the designer of the virus program: most likely an impotent adolescent, incapable of normal social relationships, and attempting to prove their own worth to themselves through these type of terrorist attacks.
>
> Never succeeding in that task (or in any other), since they have no worth, they will one day take a look at themselves and what they've done in their past, and kill themselves in disgust. This is a Good Thing, since it saves the taxpayers' money which normally would be wasted on therapy and treatment of this miscreant.
>
> If they *really* want a challenge, they'll try to destroy *my* hard disk on my BBS, instead of the disk of some innocent person. I challenge them to upload a virus or other Trojan horse to my BBS that I can't disarm. It is doubtful the challenge will be taken: the profile of such a person prohibits them from attacking those who can fight back. Alas, having a go with this lowlife would be amusing for the five minutes it takes to disarm whatever they invent.
>
> Go ahead, you good-for-nothing little slimebucket: make *my* day!

Alas, somebody out there opted to do the cowardly thing and to use the FLUSHOT programs as a vehicle for wreaking still more destruction on people like you. The FLUSHOT3 program was redistributed along with a companion program to aid you in reading the documentation. It was renamed FLUSHOT4. And the reader program was turned into a Trojan itself.

I guess the programmer involved was too cowardly to take me up on my offer and prefers to hurt people not capable of fighting back. I should have known that, I suppose, but I don't normally think of people who attack innocents. Normally, I think of people to respect, not people to pity, certainly not people who must cause such damage in order to "get off."

124

They are below contempt, obviously, and can do little to help themselves out of the mire they live in.

Still, a "worm" is a "worm."

## A Brief History

The original incarnation of FLU_SHOT was a quick hack done in my spare time. It had a couple of bugs in it which caused it to trigger when it shouldn't, and a few conditions which I had to fix. A strangeness in how COMMAND.COM processed certain conditions when I "failed" an operation caused people to lose more data than they had intended — certainly not my intent!

FLU_SHOT was modified and became FLUSHOT2. It included some additional protections, protecting some other important system files, and protecting against direct disk writes which can be used to circumvent FLUSHOT's protection mechanisms.

Additionally, FLUSHOT2 forced an exit of the program currently running instead of a fail condition when you indicated that an operation should not be carried out.

FLUSHOT2 was also now distributed in the popular archive format (have you remembered to send your shareware check in to Phil Katz for his efforts? You really should. It ain't that much money!).

Next came FLUSHOT3. A bug was fixed which could have caused certain weird things when you denied direct disk I/O to certain portions of DOS 3.x.

The enhancements to FLUSHOT3 included the ability to enter a "G" when FLUSHOT was triggered. This allowed FLUSHOT to become inactive until an exit was called by the foreground task. So, when you used some trustworthy program which did direct disk I/O, you wouldn't be pestered with constant triggering after you enter the "G". Primarily this was a quick hack to allow programs such as the FORMAT program to run without FLUSHOT being triggered each time it tried to do any work it was supposed to.

## FLU_SHOT + Features and Enhancements

This release of FLU_SHOT has a new name: FLU_SHOT +. Because FLUSHOT4 was a Trojan, I opted to change the name. Besides, FLU_SHOT + is the result of some real effort on my part, instead of being a part-time quick hack. I hope the effort shows.

FLUSHOT is now table driven. The table is in a file which I call FLUSHOT.DAT. It exists in the root directory on your C: Drive. However, I'll advise you later on how to change its location so that a "worm" can't create a Trojan to modify that file.

This file now allows you to write and/or read protect entire classes of programs. This means that you can write protect from damage all of your *.COM, *.EXE, *.BAT, and *.SYS files. You can read protect all of your *.BAT files so that a nasty program cannot even determine what name you used for FLU_SHOT+ when you invoked it!

Additionally, you can now automatically check programs when you first invoke FLU_SHOT+ to determine if they've changed since you last looked at them. Called *checksumming*, it allows you to know immediately if one of the protected programs has been changed when you're not looking. Additionally, this checksumming can even take place each time you load the program for execution.

Also, FLU_SHOT+ will advise you when any program "goes TSR." TSR stands for *Terminate and Stay Resident*, allowing pop-ups and other useful programs to be created. A "worm" could create a program which leaves a bit of slime behind. Programs like Borland's SideKick program, a wonderful program and certainly not a Trojan or virus, is probably the best known TSR. FLU_SHOT+ will advise you if any program attempts to go TSR which you haven't already registered in your FLUSHOT.DAT file.

Finally, FLU_SHOT+ will also now pop-up a little window in the middle of your screen when it gets triggered. It also will more fully explain why it was triggered. The pop-up window means that your screen won't get screwed up beyond recognition—unless you're in graphics mode when it pops up. Sorry, 'dems the breaks!

This version, FLU_SHOT+ version 1.5 has some other substantial improvements on the security side, has a couple of bug fixes here and there and is generally the same program—just a little more reliable, and a little more user friendly. And, more closely attuned to what you, the user community, have asked me for.

## Registering FLU_SHOT+

FLU_SHOT+ is not a free program. You're encouraged to use it, to distribute it to your friends and co-workers. If you end up not using it for some reason, let me know why and I'll see if I can do something about it in the next release.

But, the right to use FLU_SHOT+ is contingent upon you paying for the right to use it. I ask for ten dollars as a registration fee, plus four dollars to meet my costs for shipping, handling, and processing each order. This entitles you to get informed when the next update is available, and to have someone available to help support you with any problem you might have with the program. And it allows you to pay me, in part, for my labor in creating the entire FLU_SHOT series. I don't expect to get my normal consulting rate or to get a return equal to that of other programs which I've developed and sell through more traditional channels. That's not my intent, or I would have made FLU_SHOT + a commercial program and you'd be paying lots more money for it.

Some people are uncomfortable with the shareware concept, or believe that there ain't no such thing as Trojan or Virus programs, and that a person who profits from the distribution of a program such as FLU_SHOT must be in it for the money. Although I sympathize with their feelings, I feel that a user of FLU_SHOT simply *must* pay for their usage of the program—using it for free is paramount to stealing, and we know how wrong that is!

I've created an alternative for these folks. I'll call it "charityware" [first called that, to my knowledge, by Roedy Green]. You can also register FLU_SHOT + by sending me a check for $10 made out to your favorite charity. And a check made out to me for $4 to handle my costs. Be sure to include a stamped and addressed envelope. I'll forward the monies on to them and register you fully.

Of course, if you wish, you can send me a check for more than $14. I'll cash it gladly (I'm no fool!).

## Site Licensing of FLU_SHOT +

So, you run the computer department of a big corporation, you got a copy of FLU_SHOT +, decided it was wonderful and that it did everything you wanted and sent in your ten bucks. Then you distributed it to your 1000 users.

Not what is intended by the shareware scheme. *Each* site using FLU_SHOT + should be registered. That's ten bucks a site, me bucko! Again, make the check out to charity if you're uncomfortable with the idea of a programmer actually deriving an income from their work.

However, if you've really got 1000 computers, you should give me a call. As much as I'd like to get $10 for each site, that wouldn't be fair to you. So, quantity discounts are available.

Here's our quantity discount schedule. Remember to add in the four dollar charge for each order.

| Quantity | Price Each |
|---|---|
| 1 - 49 | $10 |
| 50 - 249 | $ 9 |
| 250 - 499 | $ 7 |
| 500 + | $ 6 |
| 10,000 + | No Charge |

Site licensee's get a "gold" disk, and make their own copies at their site, working on the honor system. Each site license does require a separate agreement, so be sure to give us a call to work out the details.

## The FLUSHOT.DAT File

FLU__SHOT+ is table driven by the contents of the FLUSHOT.DAT file. This file normally exists in the root directory of your C: drive (C:\FLUSHOT.DAT).

A little later in this document you'll see how to disguise the data filename, making life tougher for the "worms" out there. But for the purposes of this document, we'll assume that the file is called C:\FLUSHOT.DAT.

The FLU__SHOT+ program will read this data file exactly once. It reads the data from the data file into memory and overwrites the name of the data file in so doing. A little extra protection in hiding the name of the file.

This data file contains a number of lines of text. Each line of text is of the form:

<Command> = <filename> <options>

Command can be any one of the following characters:

P - Write Protect the file named
R - Read Protect the file named
E - Exclude the file named from matching P or R lines
T - The named file is a legitimate TSR
C - Perform checksum operations on the file named

The filename can be an ambiguous file if you wish for all commands except the "T" and "C" commands. This means that:

C:\level1\*.COM

128

will specify all COM files on your C: Drive in the level1 directory (or its subdirectories). Specifying:

```
C:\level1\*\*.EXE
```

would specify all EXE files in subdirectories under the C:\level1 directory, but would not include that directory itself.

You can also use the "?" operator to specify ambiguous characters as in:

```
?:\usr\bin\?.COM
```

would be used to specify files on any drive in the \usr\bin directory on that drive. The files would have to be single letter filenames with the extension of "COM".

Ambiguous filenames are not allowed for the "T" and "C" options.

## Protecting Files from Write Access

Use the "P=" option to protect files from write access. To disallow writes to any of your COM, EXE, SYS, and BAT files, specify lines of the form:

```
P = *.COM
P = *.EXE
P = *.SYS
P = *.BAT
```

which protects these files on any disk, in any directory.

## Protecting Files from Read Access

Similarly, you can use the "R" command to protect files from being read by a program (including the ability to "TYPE" a file!). To prevent read access to all of your BAT files, use a line such as:

```
R = *.BAT
```

Combinations of R and P lines are allowed, so the combination of the above lines would prevent read or write access to all batch files.

## Excluding Files

Programmers in particular should find usage for the "E" command. This allows you to exclude matching filenames from other match operations. Assume you're doing development work in the C:\develop directory. You could exclude FLU_SHOT+ from being triggered by including a line such as:

```
E = C:\develop\*.*
```

Of course, you might have development work on many disks under a directory of that name. If you do, you might include a line which looks like:

```
E = ?:\develop\*.*
        or
E = *\develop*
```

## Checksumming Files

This line is a little more complicated than others and involves some setup work. It's worth it though!

A checksum is a method used to reduce a files validity into a single number. Adding up the values of the bytes which make up the file would be a simple checksum method. Doing more complex mathematics allows for more and more checking information to be included in a test.

If you use a lie on the form:

```
C = C:\COMMAND.COM[12345]
```

then when FLU_SHOT+ first loads, it will check the validity of the file against the number in the square brackets. If the checksum calculated does not match the number presented, you'll be advised with a triggering of FLUSHOT, which presents the correct checksum.

When you first set up your FLUSHOT.DAT file, use a dummy number such as "12345" for each of the files you wish to checksum. Then, when you run FLUSHOT, you should copy down the "erroneous" checksum presented. Then, edit the FLUSHOT.DAT file and replace the dummy number with the actual checksum value you had copied down. Voila! If even one byte in there is changed, you'll be advised the next time you run FLU_SHOT+.

But wait! There's more! Not available in stores!

Sorry. I got carried away.

Seriously, there is more. When a "checksummed" file is loaded by MS-DOS, it will, by default, be checksummed again. So, if you had a line such as:

```
C = C: \ usr \ bin \ WS.COM[12345]
```

the venerable old WordStar program (still *my* editor of choice!) would be checksummed each time you went to edit a file.

Of course, you might not want the overhead of that checksumming to take place each time you load a program. Therefore, a few switches have been added. The switches are placed immediately after the "]" in the checksum line:

```
C = C: \ usr \ bin \ WS.COM[12345] < switch >
```

These switches are:

,n    Will only checksum the file only "n" times. Only one digit allowed.

–    Only checksum this file when FLU_SHOT + first loads. ",1" and " – " are equivalent.

+    Only checksum this file when it is loaded and executed, not when FLU_SHOT + first loads.

Therefore, if you wished to only check your WS.COM file when you first loaded the FLU_SHOT + program, you'd specify a line as:

```
C = C: \ usr \ bin \ ws.com[12345],1
            or
C = C: \ usr \ bin \ ws.com[12345] –
```

If you wished to checksum your program called "MY_PROG.EXE" only when it was used, try:

```
C = C: \ path \ MY_PROG.EXE +
```

## Registering a TSR Program

Any unregistered TSR program which is run after FLU_SHOT + will cause a trigger when they "go TSR." You can register a program so no trigger goes off by specifying it in a line such as:

    T = C: \ usr \ bin \ tsr__s \ sk.com

which will keep FLU__SHOT + from complaining about sk.com. Make sure to take a look at the " – T" option, specified in the next section.

## Restricted Access

Normally, when access to a file causes FLU__SHOT + to trigger, the user is given the option of hitting a "Y" to allow the access, or a "G" to allow the access until program exit or a key is hit. However, in some cases, access to a file should *never* be allowed. If you end a line in your FLUSHOT.DAT file with an "!", then the trigger will indicate that this is a restricted access file, and the user will be asked to press a key to continue. In any case, trigger accesses resulting from a line with a "!" at the end will not be allowed to go forth. For example, if you never want anyone to be able to read an AUTOEXEC.BAT file on any of your disks, have a line of the form:

    R = *AUTOEXEC.BAT!

in your FLUSHOT.DAT file. That's pretty easy! (Make sure, however, to take a look at the FSP command line arguments for the "- -" switch.)

## Protecting the FLUSHOT.DAT File

Obviously, the weak link in the chain of the protection which FLU__SHOT + offers you is the FLUSHOT.DAT file.

You would think that you'd want to protect the FLUSHOT.DAT file from reads and writes as specified above. However this, too, leaves a gaping security hole: memory could be searched for it, and it could be located that way. A better alternative exists. In the distribution package for FLUSHOT + exists a program called FLU__POKE.COM. This program allows you to specify the new name you wish to call the FLUSHOT.DAT file. Simply type:

    FLU__POKE <flushot__name>

where *<flushot_name>* represents the full path filename of your copy of FLU_SHOT+.

You'll be prompted for the name of the FLUSHOT.DAT file. Enter the name you've selected (remember to specify the disk and directory as part of the name). Voila! Nothing could be easier.

Here's an example, assuming that you've already named your FLUSHOT.DAT to FRED.TXT, and it resides in the C:\DOC directory. Assume that FSP.COM is in the current directory and has been renamed to MYFILE.COM. Here's the command line:

```
FLU_POKE MYFILE.COM
File opened ok . . .
```

Enter the FLUSHOT.DAT filename (full pathname): FRED.TXT

## Protection Recommendations

Here's a sample FLUSHOT.DAT file, basically the same one included in the archive. Your actual checksums will differ, and you may want to modify what files and directories are protected. Obviously, your exact needs are different than mine, so consider this a generic FLUSHOT.DAT:

```
P = *.bat
P = *.sys
P = *.exe
P = *.com
R = *AUTOEXEC.BAT
R = *CONFIG.SYS
E = ?\dev\*
C = C:\COMMAND.COM[12345] –
C = C:\IBMBIO.COM[12345] –
C = C:\IBMDOS.COM[12345] –
```

## Allowing "Dangerous" Programs to Run

In some cases, though, you'll still want the ability to let "trusted" programs run—even if they are potentially dangerous. A good example of this is the DOS FORMAT program: here is a program specifically designed to overwrite the data on your disk in such a way that it would be difficult, at best, to recover. Yet, the program is a necessary part of your day-to-day computer usage.

Therefore, the X = switch has been added in to allow a program such as FORMAT to run without interruption. *This is a potential security hole.* To prevent an X= program from being corrupted, I suggest you also include any X= program as both a C= and a P= program as well: any writes to the file would cause FLU_SHOT to trigger, and you wouldn't be able to run a modified program without first giving FLU_SHOT permission. Use X= sparingly. I'm rather uncomfortable with it myself.

## Running FLUSHOT+

For extra protection, after you've run FLU_POKE, you should rename the FLU_SHOT+ program that is something unique and meaningful to you, but not a "worm."

Assuming you didn't rename it, however, you could invoke the program simply by typing:

    FSP

when at the prompt. That's all there is to it. When you're satisfied, you can add it to your AUTOEXEC.BAT file, after all of your trusted programs have run. But there are some options you should know about.

## Checksumming the In-Memory Table

Since the wily "worm" may well be able to thwart some of the efforts of FLU_SHOT+ by playing nasty games with the in-memory copy of the FLUSHOT.DAT file, FLU_SHOT+ will also check this table against a checksum it generates on a regular basis. If the table gets corrupted, you'll be advised of it. This table is checked with each call to DOS, so the table must be in good shape before any disk I/O is done.

## Intercepting Direct Disk Writes Through INT13

The default operation of FLU_SHOT+ is to intercept and examine every call to the direct disk routines. You can *disable* this by including the "−F" switch on your command line:

    FSP − F

This is not recommended, but exists primarily for developers who can't use the constant triggering one of their programs may cause.

## What About INT26

Similarly, the same exists for the direct writes which normally are only made by DOS through interrupt 26. Again, I do not recommend you disable the checking, but if you desire to do so, use the " – D" switch.

## Turning Off the Header Message

If you've no desire to see the rather lengthy welcome message which is displayed when you first use FLU_SHOT + , use the " – h" switch.

## Disabling Triggering on Open with Write Access

Files which are opened with write access allowed are often not ever written to. For example, a COPY A.COM B.COM will open *both* files for write access, although DOS will not actually write to the A.COM file. Programmer laziness is the most likely excuse, and I'm as guilty of it as anyone else. However, this can cause some false alarms, which can alarm you! If you specify the " – W" switch on your command line, you won't have this particular alert come up.

Since the actual write operation to this file is also protected by FLU_SHOT + , there is no real danger with using the " – W" option—except that a "protected" file could be created anew without you being triggered. That's not too big a deal. Future versions of FLU_SHOT + will most probably have the " – W" option as the default operation.

## Changing the Trigger Window Attributes

Certain displays, particularly monochrome displays which try to emulate color displays, have a problem with the default selection of attributes in the trigger window of FLU_SHOT + . If you use the " – Axcx:yy" switch, you can modify these attributes.

The xx:yy represent the hex values (as selected from the table below) for the interior and the perimeter of the trigger window.

The "xx" represents the interior attribute, the "yy", the perimeter. If you use the " – A" switch, you *must* select both of these values—failure to do so may give a rather strange display.

What follows is a table of color and characteristics associated with the attribute byte. A byte has eight bits. Counting from the leftmost bit, the first bit of the attribute byte, if set, will cause the character to blink, regardless of other settings. The next three bits represent the background color for a given character position. The next bit indicates whether a character should have high intensity turned on. Finally, the last three bits represent the color of the character itself. To create the color of your choice, simply combine the bits, then calculate what they are in hexadecimal. If you're not sure of how to create a hexadecimal representation of a binary number, have no fear: that information follows, too.

*Bkgrnd*          *Frgrnd*

B   CLR       I   CLR

[ ]   [ ][ ][ ]   [ ]   [ ][ ][ ]

Brightness————
Background————
Intensity————
Foreground————

| Bit Pattern | | | Value | Color | Value in hex if B or I set |
|---|---|---|---|---|---|
| 0 | 0 | 0 | 0 | Black | 8 |
| 0 | 0 | 1 | 1 | Blue | 9 |
| 0 | 1 | 0 | 2 | Green | a |
| 0 | 1 | 1 | 3 | Cyan | b |
| 1 | 0 | 0 | 4 | Red | c |
| 1 | 0 | 1 | 5 | Magenta | d |
| 1 | 1 | 0 | 6 | Yellow | e |
| 1 | 1 | 1 | 7 | White | f |

For example, to create an attribute byte that is high intensity, blinking yellow characters on a green background, the attribute byte would be:

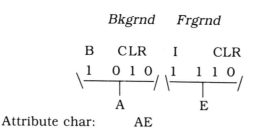

Bkgrnd     Frgrnd

B   CLR     I     CLR
1   0 1 0   1   1 1 0
A           E

Attribute char:        AE

**Important**    If the value is less than 10 (hex), you \*must\* include a leading zero or strange things will happen to the selected value.

### Allowing Trusted TSR's to Work

Normally, you'd load all of your trusted TSR's before FLUSHOT+ is loaded from within your AUTOEXEC.BAT file. However, you might want to use SideKick once in a while, removing it from memory as you desire. This could cause some problems, since SideKick, and programs like it, take over certain interrupts, and FLU_SHOT+ could get confused about whether this is a valid call or a call that shouldn't be allowed. Normally, FLU_SHOT+ will trigger on these calls, which is safer, but can be annoying. If you use the special " – T" switch upon program invocation, then calls which trusted TSR's (those specified with the T = command in your FLUSHOT.DAT file) make will be allowed. Understand, please, that this basically means that calls made by a Trojan while a trusted TSR is loaded may not be caught. Please, use this switch with caution!

### Disabling FLU_SHOT+

There may be times when you're about to do some work which you know will trigger FLU_SHOT+. And you might not want to be bothered with all of the triggering, the pop-up windows and your need to respond to each trigger. If you look in the upper right-hand corner of your screen, you'll see a " + " sign. This indicates that FLU_SHOT+ is monitoring and attempting to protect your system. Depress the ALT key three times. Notice that the " + " sign turned into a " – "? Well, FLU_SHOT+ is now disabled, and will not trigger on any event. If you depress the ALT key three more times, you'll see the " – " turn back into a " + "—each time you depress the ALT key three times, FLU_SHOT+ will toggle between being enabled and disabled.

### Disabling the Disabling of FLU_SHOT+

Yes, I know about the poor grammar used in the heading, but I couldn't think of a better way of expressing it. You can cause FLU_SHOT+ to ignore the "strike ALT three times" function discussed above. If you'd rather that the people using the machine FLU_SHOT is working on \*not\* be able to disable it, then enter the "- -" switch on the command line, as in:

    FSP - -

this is important when used in combination with the "!" restricted file access option you may have opted to use in your FLUSHOT.DAT file.

## Disabling FLU_SHOT+ Toggle Display

Alas, there are graphics applications which will be screwed up be the " – " or " + " in the upper right-hand corner of your display. Therefore, if you depress the CTRL key three times, you'll be able to toggle the display capability of FLU_SHOT+. The default configuration of FLU_SHOT+ is to "come up" with display turned on. You can reverse this capability if you include the " – G" (for graphics) switch on your command line when you run FLU_SHOT+.

When you toggle this function, the " – " or the " + " won't appear or disappear immediately. Simply that the repainting of them will no longer take place.

## Defining Your Own "Special Keys"

If you would like to, you can define your own "special keys" (as in the default Alt and Ctrl keys in a similar way as you define your attributes above. Use the " – Kxx:yy" option, which takes the hexadecimal scan code value for the replacement Alt key as the first argument (the "xx") and the hexadecimal scan code value for the replacement Ctrl key value. If you're not sure of what your scan codes are, you should look them up in your BIOS tech ref manual—or there are a multitude of programs which will print out the scan code for a given key. Most of these programs are available on BBS's throughout the world, including the Software Concepts Design, RamNet BBS at (212) 889-6438.

Due to extreme programmer fatigue, the "Welcome" message you see when you first run FLU_SHOT+ with the " – K" option will not change to reflect your selection. Maybe in the next version. And, of course, it depends upon how much you, the end-user want such an option.

**Important** If the value is less than 10 (hex), you *must* include a leading zero or strange things will happen to the selected value.

## Forcing FLU_SHOT + to Only Use the BIOS

Certain machines are not totally compatible with the IBM BIOS, which is the BIOS for which FLU_SHOT + was written. Because FLU_SHOT has to be able to deal with the hardware in a pretty direct manner in order to "pop-up" a screen, these machines were not able to use FLU_SHOT. If you specify the " – B" switch in your command line when you first run FLU_SHOT +, then only the BIOS will be used for screen output. This is *drastically* slower than direct screen memory writes (the method used unless you specify to use the BIOS), but at least it works. However, the "hit ALT and/or CTRL three times" options may not work in these machines—only your experimentation will tell.

## Putting FLU_SHOT + to Sleep When It's First Run

One of the idiosyncrasies of DOS is how a batch file is processed. Basically, DOS opens the batch file, reads the next command, closes the batch file, executes the command, and then starts over again until the batch file is exhausted of commands.

This would, normally, not be a problem, but it can become one when you opt to place the FLU_SHOT command line in your AUTOEXEC.BAT file *and* you've opted to Read Protect (with the "R =" option) the AUTOEXEC file itself: you'll be advised that some program is reading this protected file. Not a big deal, really, but certainly a hassle when you first boot up your system. Therefore, protections within FLU_SHOT are not turned on a certain amount of time. The default is set to ten seconds, or until you enter a key. You can modify the default "sleep" time by entering a " – Sn" option on the command line, where "n" represents the number of eighteenths of a second ($1/18$) you wish to have FLU_SHOT + sleep before becoming active. Since you will most likely have FLU_SHOT + as one of the final commands in your AUTO-EXEC.BAT, you probably won't have to modify this parameter, but the capability exists, nonetheless.

## Interpreting a FLU_SHOT + Trigger

So, you've run FLU_SHOT +, and you're at your C > prompt. Great! Now stick a blank disk which you don't care about into your A: Drive and try to format it.

Surprise! FLU_SHOT + caught the attempt! You have three choices now: typing "Y" allows the operation to continue, but the next one will be caught as well. Typing a "G" (for Go!) allows the operation to continue, disabling FLU__SHOT + until an exit from the program is made. When FLU__SHOT + is in the "G" state, a "G" will appear in the upper right-hand corner of your screen.

Any other key will cause a failure of the operation to occur.

When you've got FLU__SHOT + running and you get signaled that there is a problem, you should think about what might have caused the problem. Some programs, like FORMAT, or the Norton Utilities or PC-Tools, or DREP have very good reasons for doing direct reads and writes to your hard disk. However, a public domain checkbook accounting program doesn't. You'll have to be the judge of what are legitimate operations and which are questionable.

There is no reason to write to IBMBIO or IBMDOS, right? Wrong! When you format a disk with the "/S" option, those files are created on the target diskette. The act of creating, opening up and writing those files will trigger FLU__SHOT + as part of its expected operation. There are many other legitimate operations which may cause FLU__SHOT + to trigger.

So will copying a COM or EXE file if you have those protected with a "P = " command. FLU__SHOT + is not particularly intelligent about what is allowed and what isn't. That's where you, the pilot, get to decide.

Here's a fuller listing of the messages which you might see when you're using FLU__SHOT +:

    Checking  = = = >  <filename>

This message is displayed as FLU__SHOT + checks the checksum on all of the "C = " files when you first invoke FLU__SHOT + . The files must be read in from disk, their checksum calculated and then compared against the value you claim the checksum should equal.

If the checksum does *not* equal what you claim it should (which means that the file may have been written to and might therefore be suspect), a window will pop up in the middle of your screen:

    Bad Checksum on  <filename>
    Actual Checksum is:  <checksum>
Press "Y" to allow, "G" to go till exit, any other key to exit.

This message simultaneously advises you there is a problem with the checksums not matching, shows you what the checksum should be and then awaits your response.

Except for the initial run of FLU_SHOT +, if you type a "Y" or a "G", then the program will load and execute. Typing any other key will cause the program to abort and for you to be returned to the C > prompt. When FLU_SHOT + is in the "G" state, a "G" will appear in the upper right-hand corner of your screen.

If this is the initial run of FLU_SHOT +, however, you'll be advised of the program's actual checksum, but FLU_SHOT + will continue to run, checking all remaining "C =" files in the FLUSHOT.DAT file.

If you're running a program and you see a screen like:

? WARNING! TSR Request from an unregistered program!
Number of paragraphs of memory requested (in decimal) are: < cnt >
(Press any key to continue)

you're being advised that a program is about to go TSR. If this is a program you trust (such as SideKick, of KBHIT, or a host of other TSR programs you've grown to know and love), then you should consider installing a "T = " line in the FLUSHOT.DAT file so that future runs of this program will not trigger FLU_SHOT +.

However, if you get this message when running a program you don't think has any need to go TSR (such as the proverbial checkbook balancing program), you should be a little suspicious. Having a TSR program is not, in and of itself, something to be suspicious of. But having one you don't expect—well, that's a different story.

Most TSR's "hook into" an interrupt vector before they go TSR. These hooks might intercept and process key strokes ("hotkeys"), or they might hook and intercept direct disk writes themselves. In any event, FLU_SHOT + (in this version!) doesn't have the smarts to do more than advise you of the TSR'ing of the program. If you're truly suspicious, reboot your machine immediately!

If a program attempts to write directly to the interrupts which are reserved for disk writes, FLU_SHOT + will also be triggered and you'll see something like:

= = >Direct Disk Write attempt by program other than DOS! < = =
(From Interrupt <xx>)
Press "Y" to allow, "G" to go till exit, any other key to fail.

where the <xx> represents either a 13 (indicating a direct BIOS write to the disk) or a 26 (indicating a direct DOS write). Again,

141

pressing a "Y" or a "G" allows the operation to continue, pressing any other key will cause the operation to return a failed status to DOS, and the operation will not take place. When FLU__SHOT+ is in the "G" state, a "G" will appear in the upper right hand corner of your screen.

If an attempt is made to format your disk, which may be a legitimate operation made by the DOS FORMAT program, you'll see a message such as:

```
= = >Disk being formatted! Are You Sure?< = =
Press "Y" to allow, "G" to go till exit, any other key to fail.
```

which follows similarly to the direct disk write operations. You should question whether the format operation is appropriate at the time and take whatever action you think is best.

If one of your protected files is about to be written to, you'll see a message like:

```
Write access being attempted on:
<filename>
Press "Y" to allow, "G" to go till exit, any other key to fail.
```

where <filename> represents the file you're trying to protect from these write operations. Your red flag should fly, and you should question why the program currently running should cause such an operation.

You may also see the same type of message when one of your "Read-Protected" files is being accessed:

```
Read Access being attempted on:
<filename>
Press "Y" to allow, "G" to go till exit, any other key to fail.
```

Again, the same red flag should fly, but it doesn't mean that you're infected with some nasty virus program! It could be something harmless or intended. You'll have to be the judge.

```
Open File with Write access being attempted on:
<filename>
Press "Y" to allow, "G" to go till exit, any other key to fail.
```

If you see the above message: Don't Panic! When a program

opens a file, it may open the file for different types of access. One access method prohibits writing to the file. Another allows you to write to the file. However, lazy programmers (myself included in this category from time to time) will often open a file for read *and* write access, even though they have no intention of ever doing a write into the file. FLU_SHOT + isn't smart enough to be able to figure out what a program *might* do in the future, so it will alert you to an attempt to open the indicated protected file with write access allowed. Again, you'll have to consider whether the program opening the file is a "trusted" program or not and you'll have to then decide what action to take.

```
Handle Write Access being attempted on:
  <filename>
Press "Y" to allow, "G" to go till exit, any other key to fail.
```

If you see this message, it means that some program is trying to write to a protected file through an access method known as "handle access." This should normally never happen, with the caveats raised above in the "Open With Write Access" section.

There are three separate messages you'll see if a program attempts to rename a protected file (you'll only see one of these messages at a time, though):

```
FCB Rename being attempted on source file:
FCB Rename being attempted on target file:
Handle Rename being attempted on:
  <filename>
Press "Y" to allow, "G" to go till exit, any other key to fail.
```

This indicates what type of operation is attempting to rename a protected file. FCB's are a relic of the older CP/M days, and "handles" are a newer concept, a little more modern. In any event, this tells you that a file is being renamed. It is possible that a Trojan or virus writer will attempt to rename an existing protected file to some other name, then rename a Trojaned or virused program in its stead. FLU_SHOT will alert you to this action: again, though, you'll have to decide what to do about it.

```
Delete being attempted on:
  <filename>
Press "Y" to allow, "G" to go till exit, any other key to fail.
```

143

Pretty much self-evident as to what's happening here, there are very few reasons why one of the files you've opted to protect should be deleted.

## How Good is FLUSHOT +, Really?

FLU_SHOT + is a pretty handy piece of code. But, it can't absolutely protect you from a "worm." No software can do that. There are ways around FLU_SHOT +. I'm of two minds about discussing them, since the "worms" out there are reading this, too. So I'll only discuss them in passing. And I'll tell you what I use here to protect myself from "worms." First, though, a little story to tell you what it's like here, and how I protect myself from getting wormed.

The RamNet Bulletin Board System site I run is open access. No need to register, or to leave your phone number or address, although a note to that effect is always appreciated. As mentioned above, I dare the "worm" to try to affect the disk of somebody who can fight back. A couple of "worms" have tried and I have a nice collection of Trojans and viruses. Obviously, I run FLU_SHOT + on my board, along with checking incoming files with CHK4BOMB. My procedure for testing out newly uploaded code involves me doing a backup, installing all sorts of software to monitor what is going on, and doing a checksum on all files on the disk. I then try out all of the code I get, primarily to determine if the code is of high enough quality to be posted. After testing out all of the weeks uploads, I run the checksum program again to determine if any of my files might have been modified by a "worm's" virus program.

Recently, what looked like a decent little directory lister was posted to the board. For some reason I've yet to fathom, directory aid programs seem to be the ones which have the highest percentage of Trojans attached to them.

This directory aid program listed my directories in a wonderful tree structure, using different colors for different types of files. Nice program. When it exited, however, it went out and looked for a directory with the word "FLU" in it. Once it found a directory with a match in it, it proceeded to try to erase all of the files in that directory. An assault! No big deal. That's what backups are for.

But it brings up an interesting point: I was attacked by a clever "worm," and it erased a bunch of files which were pretty valuable. All of the protection I had would have been for naught if I didn't use the first line of defense from these "worms": full and adequate backup.

I've spent three years of my life developing one particular software package. Imagine what would have happened if that had been erased by a "worm"! Fortunately, I make backups at least once a day, and usually more frequently than that. You should, too.

Now, I quarantine that machine as well. I spent a couple of dollars and bought a bunch of bright red floppy disks. The basic rule around here is that Red Disks are the only disks that go into the BBS machine, and the Red Disks go into no other machine.

You see, I *know* that there is some "worm" out there who is gonna find some way to infect my system. No matter what software protection I use, there *is* a way around it.

You needn't be concerned though—you're making backups on a regular basis, right? And, you aren't asking for trouble. I am, I expect to find it, and it is sort of amusing to see what the "worms" out there are wasting their efforts on.

At this point, Trojans and viruses are becoming a hobby with me: watching what the "worms" try to do, figuring out a way to defend against it, and then updating the FLU_SHOT series.

However, there is a possibility that the FLU_SHOT series (as well as other protection programs which are just as valuable) are causing an escalation of the terms of this war. The "worms" out there are sick individuals. They must enjoy causing the damage they do. But they haven't the guts to stand up and actually do something in person. They prefer to hide behind a mist of anonymity.

But you have the ultimate defense! No, not the FLU_SHOT+ program. *FULL AND ADEQUATE BACKUPS!*

There are a variety of very good backup programs which can save you more work than you can imagine. I use the FASTBACK+ program, which is a great little program. I backup 30Megs once in a while, and do an incremental backup on a very frequent basis. There are a variety of very good commercial, public domain, and shareware backup programs out there. Use them! Because, no matter what software protection you use, somebody will find a way around it one day. But they can't find a way around your backups. And, if you (and everyone else) do regular backups, you'll remove the only joy in life these "worms" have. They'll kill themselves, hopefully, and an entire subspecies will be wiped out — and you'll be partially responsible!

My advance thanks for helping to exterminate these little slimebuckets. But that brings me to something else.

## Reward Offered

Somebody out there knows who the "worms" are. Even they must have someone who is a friend. True, I can't think of any reason someone would befriend a "worm." But somebody who doesn't know better has.

Well, I'm offering a reward for the capture and conviction of these "worms."

Enough already with software protection schemes, hardware protection schemes, or any protection at all. It shouldn't be required!

Here's the deal:

In this archive is a form called REWARD.FRM. If you're a software or hardware manufacturer, or you have some software or hardware you don't need, consider filling out that form, and donating it to a worthy cause. I don't know what the legal and tax ramifications of that donation would be. I'm not a lawyer and we can cross that bridge when we get to it.

Anyway, if you know one of these "worms," turn them in! Call me up, send me a letter, a telegram, or leave a message for me on my BBS. Indicate who you *know* is worming about. I'll keep your name confidential.

It is surprisingly easy to get the authorities in on this—they're as concerned about what is happening to our community as we are. I'll presume that they'll end up putting a data tap on the phone line of the accused "worm." Then, when he next uploads a Trojan or a virus to a BBS, he'll get nailed. The authorities are pretty good about this stuff: they'll not tap a phone or take any action whatsoever without adequate proof. Will your dropping a dime on this "worm" be adequate proof? I don't know. Again, a bridge to cross when we approach it.

However, assuming that this slimeball gets nailed, you'll get all of the software and hardware which other people have donated. And the satisfaction of knowing that you've done a Good Thing, that you've helped an industry and community continue to grow. This *is* your community, and the vast majority of people in it are good people who shouldn't have to fear from your friend. Your friend is not really a friend: he uses you to justify his own existence. When someone uses you like that, they're not a friend, they're a leech. And you've probably got better things to do then let somebody use you like that.

Most importantly, the "worm" out there won't know if one of his friends has already turned him in. So he won't know if his phone

```
------------------------------------------------------------------------
          FLU_SHOT+ (V1.5) Registration

Please fill out this form, then mail it along with a check for
$14 ($10 Registration, $4 Shipping/Handling/Processing) (or
more!) to:

                Ross M. Greenberg
                Software Concepts Design
                594 Third Avenue
                New York, New York 10016


Thanks for your support!

Name:_____

Title:_____

Company:_____

Address:_____

        _____

City:    _____     State: _____  Zip:_____

Telephone:_____

Comments and Suggestions:_____

        _____

        _____

        _____

        _____


Where did you get FLUSHOT+ (V1.5) from? (check one, fill in the blank):

        [__]   User Group  (which one:_____)

        [__]   BBS  (Name:_____)(Tel #:_____)

        [__]   Other (Such as:_____)


Please send me more information on:

        [__]   RamNet, the background communications program

        [__]   The Programmer's Co_operative

------------------------------------------------------------------------
```

is tapped. If *I* were a "worm," and considering what kind of friends I would have, I'd be sure that somebody dropped a dime on me. And therefore an intelligent "worm" (perhaps I'm giving the "worm" too much credit?) must presume that their line is tapped and that they're gonna go to jail if they continue what they're doing.

So just stop, you miserable little lowlife, huh? You're going to be arrested. You're going to have to put up with indignities which even you don't deserve! Your equipment will be confiscated. You'll never get a job in the industry. You're going to go to jail.

All because one of your friends actually has a conscience and knows what is right and what is wrong. And what you're doing is wrong.

So, let me get back to the kind of programming I enjoy —productive programming. And turn your programming to useful, interesting, and productive programming. You have the talent to do something useful and good with your life. What you're doing is hurting the industry and hurting the community which would welcome someone with your talents with open arms.

And the satisfaction of helping far surpasses the satisfaction you must get from hurting innocent people.

So just stop.

Sincerely, Ross M. Greenberg

## CBIN2

### CBN2.EXE

### by Steven Stern 70327 ,135

CBIN.EXE is a program to compare, byte for byte, two files. CBIN v2.0 will compare each byte, to the end-of-file of the longer of the two files or for a specified number of differences. Type CBIN for command syntax. This program is self-documenting.

## DPROTECT

### DPROTECT version 1.03, 07/07/86

©1985, 1986, GEE WIZ™ Software Company

by Gee M. Wong

*A disk protection scheme*

148

## Notice

DPROTECT may not be sold, used in a commercial environment, nor packaged with any commercial product without prior written permission from GEE WIZ Software Company.

DPROTECT may be distributed freely at no cost to the recipient. User support for this utility may be best obtained by notifying GEE WIZ. *No subscription is necessary for user support.*

If you feel that this utility is of value, please feel free to send your voluntary contribution of $5.00 to:

> Gee M. Wong
> 6 South Woodland Avenue
> East Brunswick, NJ 08816

## Description

DPROTECT may be used to write protect one or more floppy disk drives and all fixed disk drives from Trojan horse programs. DPROTECT may not be capable of protecting any RAM disk or external/network drives which do not resemble a standard IBM floppy disk or hard disk drive.

DPROTECT has been tested on a 3270-PC, XT/370, and AT/370 equipped with the standard floppy disk and hard disk drives and controllers supplied by IBM, using PC-DOS™ 2.1, 3.1, and 3.2.

When DPROTECT is executed, it will install a portion of itself as a resident program, and it will redirect all invocations of BIOS level interrupt 13H to its resident code, which will validate all disk I/O requests.

Every time an I/O request is made, DPROTECT will intercept the request at the BIOS level, interrupt 13H, and determine if the request is being made against a drive it is protecting. If the request is being performed is against a protected drive, then the requested is analyzed to determine if the request is for a service which will modify any data on that drive. When both conditions are present, DPROTECT will display a message on the screen informing you of a detected update request, and its intention to perform a cold system reboot. Then DPROTECT will pause, to allow you enough time to read the error message, and wait for you to type any key before rebooting your PC.

For your protection, a cold system reboot is always performed whenever a drive is illegally accessed; you can never know what time bombs a Trojan horse program will leave behind in your PC's RAM or device registers.

This version of DPROTECT is only able to intercept an I/O request at a BIOS level. *DPROTECT is not able to safeguard against programs which access code in ROM through its ROM address.* Hopefully, an interpretative version of DPROTECT will be available to circumvent those Trojan horse programs which attempt to execute ROM code directly.

Once the fixed disk drives or diskette drives are protected, the only way to remove the protection is to reboot DOS.

## Usage

To protect a disk or diskette, use the command:

```
DPROTECT drive
```

where *drive* is the letter of the drive you would like to have write-protected, or * for all drives.

## Disclaimer

The author has taken due care in developing and testing the effectiveness of this utility, and makes no expressed or implied warranty of any kind with regard to this utility. In no event shall the author or GEE WIZ Software Company be liable for incidental or consequential damages in connection with or arising out of the use of this utility.

| Version | Date | Description of Changes |
|---------|------|------------------------|
| 1.00 | 10/01/85 | NONE. This is the original version. |
| 1.01 | 10/11/85 | Corrected code which performs system reboot to force a COLD boot. The original version was accidentally released with code for performing a WARM boot. |
| 1.02 | 11/07/85 | Improved the code which scans the command line to allow for multiple spaces, and to verify that a drive letter was specified. If no drive letter was used, or if the character |

specified is not a valid letter, then a short description will be generated.

1.03     07/07/86   Documentation changes.

## Notes

GEE WHIZ is a trademark of GEE WIZ Software Company.
PC-DOS is a trademark of Microsoft Incorporated.
PC-DOS is a trademark of International Business Machines.

## UNDEL

## UNDEL.COM

This program will undelete *most* files. One particularly important point: you should *not* write to that disk since deleting the file because you may inadvertently reuse some of the disk space you might want to recover.

To use, type UNDEL [d:]filename[.ext]. For ASCII files, you may use a /A switch to confirm each cluster before it is appended to the file being restored. Use only with DOS 2.0 or greater double-sided disks.

For more information, see the April 2, 1985 edition of *PC Magazine*, page 225. The article is by Steven Holzner.

You should, as always, become familiar with this program and make sure it works by experimenting with some files that aren't important.

# Index

# Index

# Index

# Index